"This is pure Sam Culbert! And, if you've never had a class with him, this book will give you that experience. He's known for his straight talk, and also for his ability to call attention to the truth of any situation. He calls it as he sees it and he seems to always be able to see what can't quite be seen. You'll probably take issue with some (or much!) of what he says, but you will appreciate the points he makes even if you want to argue the other side. Open this book and walk into his classroom!"
—**Beverly Kaye, founder, Career Systems International and co-author of** *Love 'Em or Lose 'Em: Getting Good People to Stay* **and** *Help Them Grow or Watch Them Go: Career Conversations Employees Want*

"Samuel Culbert is one of those rare writers on management who really can see the forest despite all the organizational trees. The result is *Good People, Bad Managers*—a wonderfully clear, lively, and entertaining indictment of companies and the people who run them. His 'tell it like it is' writing style is refreshingly honest and direct, as he delivers no-nonsense wisdom about just how bad most managers really are. It's a good read for managers willing to wonder why they do what they do and whether they could do it better."
—**Harold Edwards, President, CEO and Director, Limoneira**

"A String of Pearls. Muckraker, author, professor, researcher Samuel Culbert has written a career capstone, easy to read book that everyone, today's managers and managers of the future, can learn from. He gives common sense advice and puts into words what takes place every day that people totally miss."
—**Gordon Perkin, Co-founder and President of PATH, initial Director of Global Health for Bill and Melinda Gates Foundation (now retired), and recipient of the Order of Canada**

"Professor Culbert digs deep into what our Gallup research continues to show—that very few employees here in the USA and around the world are engaged in their jobs. Good People, Bad Managers gets into the guts of how this all came to be, and what managers and organizations can do to blow it up and replace it with culture and systems that support good people being good managers too."
—**Larry Emond, Managing Partner, Gallup**

"Instead of offering quick fixes, Culbert portrays the gritty reality that distracts well-intentioned managers and sets them on a self-absorbed course of mediocrity. It's a must-read for anyone, anywhere in an organization, who wants to be effective and empathetic, and for skeptics of management theory to understand the importance of knowing how other people think and why they behave as they do."
—**Gayla Kraetsch Hartsough, President of KH Consulting Group; Adjunct Associate Professor of International Public Policy, University of Southern California**

"As a former student of Sam Culbert's, and now as a business leader, I know how crucial—and difficult—it is to create open and direct discourse in a company. *Good People, Bad Managers* provides managers with the framework to do just that. The process is not for the timid, but if you care about the health and success of your organization, this provocative and thoughtful book is a must read."
—**Chip Robertson, Co-managing Director, Warland Investments Company**

GOOD PEOPLE,
BAD MANAGERS

GOOD PEOPLE, BAD MANAGERS

HOW WORK CULTURE CORRUPTS GOOD INTENTIONS

SAMUEL A. CULBERT

OXFORD
UNIVERSITY PRESS

OXFORD

UNIVERSITY PRESS

Oxford University Press is a department of the University of Oxford.
It furthers the University's objective of excellence in research, scholarship,
and education by publishing worldwide. Oxford is a registered
trade mark of Oxford University Press in
the UK and certain other countries.

Published in the United States of America by Oxford University Press
198 Madison Avenue, New York, NY 10016, United States of America.

Library of Congress Cataloging-in-Publication Data
Names: Culbert, Samuel A., author.
Title: Good people, bad managers : how work culture
corrupts good intentions / Samuel A. Culbert.
Description: New York, NY : Oxford University Press, [2017]
Identifiers: LCCN 2016035233 | ISBN 9780190652395
(jacketed hardcover : alk. paper)
Subjects: LCSH: Management. | Supervisors. | Executives. |
Executive ability. | Corporate culture. | Organizational behavior.
Classification: LCC HD31 .C79 2017 | DDC 306.3/6—dc23 LC record
available at https://lccn.loc.gov/2016035233

1 3 5 7 9 8 6 4 2

Printed by Sheridan Books, Inc., United States of America

Rosella

CONTENTS

FOREWORD

In October 1988, I was summoned to the office of Maurice "Mo" Hickey, publisher of the *Denver Post*.

Hickey was blunt. He said he'd just fired the business news editor and that the position was now vacant. Then, he offered the job to me—a wisecracking, irreverent reporter with no experience managing anything.

Chuck Green, the editor-in-chief, was in charge of my training, which lasted roughly thirty seconds. He said: "Pick a story to run at the top of the page and put a big headline on it. Put a story with a photo in the center, another story on the right, and briefs on the left." Then he added: "You'll figure out the rest."

That was it. I was now a manager. Fifteen people who were beer-drinking buddies became direct reports. What in hell was I supposed to do for them, with them, and to them? I had all the power, but was being in charge the same thing as being a manager? I didn't have a clue.

It took a while, but I eventually learned quite a bit about managing—at the *Post*, then at the *Denver Business Journal*, where I was editor-in-chief, and then at my own start-up, the *Pacific Coast Business Times*. The main thing I've learned is that to be a good manager, you need to be more than in charge. You need to be self-aware. You need to be tuned into the people who report to you—I mean, really tuned in. And you need to accept that you don't have all the answers.

Fortunately, I've had someone in my corner, someone whose life work involves untangling the complex relationships between managers and their direct reports.

That person is Samuel Culbert, the author of this book. I met him years ago, when we were introduced at a reception for the Gerald Loeb Awards at the UCLA Anderson School of Management, where he is a leader in his field of organizational development. We struck up a conversation that's continued for years over dinners, via email, and on the telephone. Throughout those years, Sam has taught me how to be a good manager, in spite of myself. He's taught me that being a good manager isn't about being a good guy or a bad guy. He's taught me that being a good manager isn't about having a vision and imposing that vision on everybody. And he's taught me that bad management behavior begins with mistaken assumptions made about people in general, and individually with each unique person encountered.

What Sam does so well is observe. He understands workplace behaviors, motivations, and consequences, both intended and unintended. He is relentless in his pursuit of straight talk. That's what this book does so well: it's a groundbreaking effort to understand and bridge the psychological gaps that are among the biggest roadblocks to success in every workplace.

I must add one note of caution. This is not a pop-culture, feel-good book where you put marks on a checklist or download an app and suddenly become a better manager in a transformed workplace. If only it were that easy. The thesis of *Good People, Bad Managers: How Work Culture Corrupts Good Intentions* is that underlying workplace problems can only be addressed by a new mind-set—held by bosses and employees alike. Sam argues that it takes an enormous commitment to throwing out much of what we've learned about how to be a manager, and thinking, perhaps for the first time, like a human being.

In pursuit of change, *Good People, Bad Managers* journeys deep inside the heads of managers and their direct reports to understand what makes them tick. Sam argues forcefully that managers are "engulfed in a cultural force-field that often has them disoriented—engaged in actions having consequences they need to be aware of and do more about." He also argues that disorientation starts early and never lets up, even in business school. No wonder there are so many bad managers: they have no clue how to be any other way!

If anybody can dissect, tear apart, and then rebuild the way managers think and behave, it is Sam—the systems engineer turned clinical psychologist. He has spent his career analyzing and deconstructing management problems at any number of corporations—from agribusinesses to giant consumer companies. He has keen powers of observation, which he has brought to bear on power and relationships in the twenty-first-century workplace. His conclusions will both shock and absorb you. His solutions will point you in new directions as you think through how to achieve your team's goals. He will make you see what management is all about in a way you've never done before. It may be disheartening at times, but it will always be enlightening.

Sam's prescription for righting what is wrong couldn't come at a more crucial time. We live in an era where bad management doesn't just lead to stress, disorientation, and weak performance. It can, and often does, lead directly to the disasters that are covered daily in the financial press. And those disasters, with the accompanying lack of responsibility at the top, are increasingly the reason why rank-and-file workers feel they are falling further and further behind, both financially and spiritually.

Imagine what would have happened inside the halls of Volkswagen if honest and intelligent communication had carried the day when management came up with the idea of short-cutting emissions tests on diesel engines.

Imagine, too, what would have happened if a culture of straight talk had prevailed a decade ago at the leading rating agencies, Moody's and Standard & Poor's. A major tragedy of the financial crisis is that management incentivized and pressed staff to sign off on triple-A ratings for billions and billions of dollars of soon-to-be worthless mortgage securities. Nobody dared to question why those ratings were being given on worthless junk, and partly because of that breakdown the world's financial markets seized up and teetered on the edge of collapse.

In *Good People, Bad Managers*, Samuel Culbert teaches us how to build better companies in America and around the world from the inside out. But we must be open-minded—and be prepared to learn hard lessons.

Henry Dubroff
CEO and Editor-in-Chief
Pacific Coast Business Times

GOOD PEOPLE, BAD MANAGERS

Part I
WHAT'S GOING ON?

1

TIME TO FACE IT

BAD MANAGEMENT IS THE NORM

Most people think that American managers are the best on the planet, and it's easy to see why. Once a person concludes that US companies are the world's most innovative and profitable, it stands to reason their managers must be incredibly smart and people-savvy.

If you're not persuaded, people around the globe seem thoroughly convinced.[1] From Shanghai to London, American managers are esteemed for their personal dynamism, entrepreneurial guile, inventive marketing, and canny leveraging of capital. Even when some lapse in judgment or dishonest act is exposed, few outsiders start thinking there might be something fundamentally wrong with how US companies are being managed. No, in the eyes of the world, the acumen of American managers is unparalleled in the history of modern times.

That's not the way I see it. I see bad management as the norm, and I've got plenty of company in seeing it this way.[2] Bad management takes place much too often to be considered an exception.

Just because a corporation makes a lot of money for its shareholders, or a nonprofit stays within budget, doesn't mean its employees are receiving the kind of guidance, support, and encouragement they need. Just because a manager graduates from an elite MBA school doesn't mean that when tested with real-life situations this person will act out the high-quality answers given attempting to earn an A on the final exam.[3]

While there are many reasons for believing American companies are the world's most successful, the character and quality of management their employees receive should not be counted as one of them.[4] Despite the halo cast by financial success, the daily human toll is despicable. What's more, it detracts from the bottom line.

I'm not talking about every company. We've all heard about the excitement people feel working in start-ups, and the feelings of well-being and community that can take place working in a small business with considerate and appreciative owners on site.

I'm talking about the experiences people are having in the majority of companies and organizations and, with a few noteworthy exceptions, in just about every large company and bureaucracy that exists. You know, the places where the preponderance of people are employed. I'm talking about the tenor of the workplace where your children and grandkids are headed. Think about it: How many jobs do you know of that you'd wish on someone you love? Someone whose sensibilities you care about, a person looking to the workplace to realize their ambitions, and for support in living a good life.

I find it a real shame that so many people are the recipients of state-of-the-art, default-setting, bad management behavior.[5] It's a shame because, for the most part, the bad behavior is meted out by well-intentioned, good people acting without realizing the negatives their actions inflict, and without awareness of the forces driving those actions. In their minds, they're doing their very best to cope with situations not of their making.

Well, at least they realize the situations in which they find themselves aren't of their making. But that hasn't been enough to provide clear vision. Bad management behavior is coming from well-educated people, including the best and the brightest America has. I'm not talking about mean-spirited people acting selfishly. I'm talking about good people, who mean well, screwing up predictably.

I wish I were wrong in sizing up the situation. Unfortunately, my beliefs are supported by what managers and other professionals tell me, and corroborated by almost every focus group and published research study. Most damning is the Gallup polling that annually concludes that four out of five people in management positions lack "the talents" to manage others effectively.[6] What are those missing talents? Gallup gives long explanations that I interpret as managers lacking the interest and capacity to give direct reports the focus needed for them to perform at their best.

What's the difference, you might ask? Companies are succeeding. And besides, notwithstanding an occasional awfulness, people have adapted to what they receive. That's right, people are inured to the bad management behavior they receive, and managers are unaware of the bad behavior they dish out. Why worry about a situation that's working fine the way it is?

I'll tell you why we should worry. Not only does bad management take a dispiriting toll on people, but, as a consequence, their companies' shareholders are losing out. The bottom lines may be profitably green, but they're not nearly as green as they ought to be. As it is, the money paid to managers is a major expense that burdens profits. Better management won't cost any more, and the efficiencies realized, and ingenuity gained, can only make profits rise.[7]

Compared to the rest of the world, American companies have some very big advantages. Relatively unencumbered by bureaucracy, they are allowed by the government to make personnel changes, to enjoy tax advantages, exploit loopholes, change business practices, sell off what no longer makes sense, and generally behave in ways the rest of the world finds efficient, even ruthless, taking a straight-line path to the end results they seek. Add to this the fact that America serves as a magnet for attracting the world's talent.

It's a travesty that being employed by the world's most successful companies should come at a cost to the well-being and sensibilities of the people performing the work. Think how much more efficient companies would be if their employees were free of unnecessary distractions, not intimidated by their managers, better able to speak their views with candor, and free to pour more of their hearts and souls into what they do. Then add in the enhanced effectiveness that will emerge when managers shift their focus to make more boss-report camaraderie possible. It sounds enticing, if you ask me—whether you are in it for well-being or bottom line.

Yet good management is advertised and promoted everywhere! Each year brings new bestsellers about how to manage people effectively, and thousands of vanity speeches by high-profile executives advising companies to go about it the way they did. So much would be different if only managers in the audience were able to implement the advice they receive. Unfortunately, they aren't able to, and employees know it. Especially in large companies, people are quick to recognize that the good management they're told they're receiving is someone's illusion, and definitely not their own reality.

I hear a new bad management account almost daily. If I don't read about one in the paper or see it on TV, then I hear it directly from some manager or professional who feels their effectiveness and well-being threatened by a bad management situation they're unable to fix. Only when a situation becomes especially egregious does the world hear the truth about what actually transpires in the workplace. Hearing what's taken place, people complain and vent their outrage. But seldom do I hear anyone saying they were surprised. It seems people actually expect to hear about problems caused by managers behaving badly.

Wait a minute. Did you catch that? People aren't surprised; in fact, they *expect* bad management! I find this alarming—because it's true. Yet, if you inquire, and I do all the time, you'd find most managers are extremely well-intentioned. Oh, if only good intentions were enough!

There's something systemic throwing them off, and managers haven't figured out what it is. Even if they knew, they'd have a hard time owning up—which is another part of the problem. Explaining what's erroneous in conventional managerial thinking, and why it goes undetected, is a big part of the understanding I'm out to provide.

Listening to the stories, one can't help but wonder what causes managers to behave in ways that arouse so many suspicions, and so much insecurity. How can managers say they're practicing good management while their direct reports plainly see so many managerial actions preventing them from being their effective selves? There's a research study[8] that investigated the managerial actions professional-level employees found most useful in their quests to work at peak effectiveness. The study concludes that the most useful thing a manager can do is not interrupt when an employee considers him- or herself to be working productively—often by calling what the employee deems a needless meeting. In other words, given the managerial *help* employees see themselves receiving, they'd prefer their managers to leave them alone.

People come to work wanting to feel good about themselves, and count on their manager to help them be their best. They come expecting to be on a path to realizing life goals. But this is not what people often enough experience. In fact, on any given day, usually without recognizing what they're going through, employees find themselves on the defensive, putting almost as much energy into getting their boss to value their contributions as they put into doing the work itself. Instead of leaving work feeling energized by what they've learned and accomplished, too many people leave feeling beat up, drained, dispirited, and emotionally needy.

No one wants management left the way it is, and that includes most managers. It doesn't have to be this way, but even if nothing were to change, it's certainly better to realize what's causing so much bad management behavior, and why it persists. Without this understanding, people don't see the inevitable coming, and lack the means to protect themselves when it hits. As it is now, they allow their expectations for good management to rise and, from my vantage point, take their disappointments much too personally. It's an ill-will situation that needs to go away.

Disenchantment in the Land of Plenty

People begin their jobs with flame, turned on, and looking to realize their potential. They want to work efficiently, the way they're best able. They expect to have assignments that leave room for them to pursue what's important in their lives. They want to grow and develop in personally meaningful directions—not the direction stipulated by a manager making self-serving assumptions about what's best for them. Feeling misunderstood and misdirected, the inner flame begins to flicker.

A great deal more affects an individual at work than can be discerned merely by observing their behavior—especially when you consider the masks people feel compelled to wear. What managers call "human capital" is so much more than interchangeable resources to be deployed for company return. These resources are precious, sensitive people with distinctive skills and limitations who want to accomplish things, and to progress in their lives for doing so. People work to enrich themselves, to learn, and to have high-quality interactions. They work to fulfill ambitions. They come with good health they'd like to preserve. You want to know how what goes on at work affects the human psyche and spirit? Just ask the people at home to whom employees return each day. Ask enough and I bet you'll conclude, as I have, that what goes on at work affects every aspect of a person's being.[9]

Unfortunately, for reasons to be explained, managers are so consumed with getting work accomplished that they feel forced to ignore whatever they can put off—and usually what can be put off most easily is attending to the needs of the people reporting to them. Managers ignore how many hours it takes to get an assignment completed, and don't want to hear about people feeling forced to put in hours off-the-clock. They use the carrot of advancement, and the stick of evaluation, to get reports to perform in ways that accrue to their success. An example of precisely what I'm describing is found in an angst-filled email sent to me by a middle manager who's seen as an "up-and-comer" in his company. Here's what he wrote that his boss knows nothing about.

I'm beginning to realize how many factors affect me at work trying to prove myself deserving a promotion. I'm always nodding my head trying to show people I'm responsive. But too often I don't retain what a person tells me because I'm always absorbed trying to get them to finish so I can get on with my work. Even bringing work home there's never enough time to catch up. It's as if I'm always picking flowers but clueless to their smell. Worst of all, I see my marriage suffering. Even in the same room, both my wife and I feel a distance. As a stay-at-home mother her stresses build as the day progresses. By the time I walk in the door, she's ready to crash. Then she needs my help checking our boys' homework and getting them bathed and ready for bed—which, after working a long day, always drains me. At home I'm impatient just like I am at work. Then there are the phone calls and emails that I exchange on weekends. I feel guilty not being the father my children need. I don't want them growing up like I had to with working parents who had little time to get involved. Telling my wife and boys I'm doing it for the family only gets me empty stares.

Specifics notwithstanding, I don't find this situation unusual. Another well-intentioned person looking to move up, and giving his job what he thinks it requires. He's got a higher-level manager, probably in a troublesome situation of their own, who has little idea of what he's going through. And what do you think people reporting to this impatient manager, who has difficulty retaining what he's told, receive in the way of help and support? Do you think his reports get better focus than he receives from his boss, or his family receives from him? With the pressures he's under, I'm guessing no one gets what they need, and everyone feels deprived. And we're talking about good people!

Could it be that not complaining and just putting up with workplace intrusiveness has become the *badge of honor* for moving up in management? Apparently, that's what many people holding high-stature, big-paying jobs seem to assume they should get from their lower-down reports. I've met several top-level executives who see nothing wrong with having key personnel on speed dial, reachable at any hour, any day— even when on vacations with their families.

But Must It Be This Way?

Everyone knows getting ahead entails trade-offs. In fact, most people expect employees with ambitions to go above and beyond whatever is required. But managers who don't know the trade-offs their reports are making, or the consequences they hold for them, lack the wherewithal for knowing if either the company or the sacrificing individual is getting good value back for what they exchange. And just like the boss of the manager who wrote that email, few managers have the means for knowing precisely what their reports see them requiring. Is it unreasonable to expect managers to have the time and inclination to learn about an employee's life so that they can realize the implications of their own words and actions? Most people I've surveyed don't believe their manager knows much of anything about the life predicaments that arise for them because of job commitments. Posed the question, "What difference would it make if your boss knew more about how your work affects your life?" the majority speculate they'd get no empathy or relief if they should ever *misspeak* by making their truths known.

Going to work shouldn't dampen the human spirit. It never does when people feel they're working effectively, have their manager's support, are appreciated, and see themselves making progress toward personally important goals. In fact, under the right circumstances, work isn't even work; it's what a person wants to be doing. But given the lack of managerial focus most people receive, those right circumstances are seldom present. People should feel happy going to work, not miserable when Sunday night rolls around and they start thinking about what's ahead for them in the morning.

It's tragic that so many employees consider their jobs an onerous obligation when, with the right kind of managerial support, a job could be become a self-valued activity. What's preventing bosses from giving employees what they actually need?

It's in the Air

I believe I've had good success helping managers to see the negatives in the management practices I've investigated, and the misguided thinking that went into conceiving them. But I haven't been nearly as successful helping managers overcome the forces that resist their changing what I've helped them to see as inappropriate and wrong. In the process of trying, I've learned a great deal about these forces, and believe I now have the prime contributor identified. What I've learned also accounts for why bad management behavior goes unrecognized by so many, and, for those who do see it, too perilous to fight.

Let me divulge what I'll be elaborating on throughout this book. The root cause of most of the bad management behavior taking place today, to which so many well-intentioned managers are oblivious, is that the American work culture, en masse, has managers thinking incorrectly. That's right. I believe most of what accounts for the failure by so many managers to live out their good intentions is caused by the very work culture so many people believe the world at large should emulate.

The American work culture leads managers to implement practices that contradict basic facts of human nature—about how people think, communicate, and function. Worse yet, the culture encourages managers to support practices that prevent everyone, themselves included, from speaking about these contradictions, and the personal binds created for them by the way their companies are managed. Even when top-level managers encourage candor from below, they don't remove the obstacles that prevent people from speaking their truths. It's enough to give one the impression that, deep down, top-level managers are only interested in hearing that everything is going along just fine. And often, that's what they do hear when they ask their employees. But that doesn't make it so.

Allow me to explain how I arrived at this conclusion. America's workforce is supposed to consist of individualistic, positive-thinking people who pick themselves up by their bootstraps and always look for the next opportunity to improve, and climb the ranks by doing so. People are so familiar with stories of individuals who have overcome huge obstacles that it's commonplace to think anyone can push themselves to master almost anything. Consequently, managers have unrealistic expectations. They think they can sweet-talk, manipulate, and intimidate employees to improve on almost any behavior they want changed. Well, they are wrong. Some things in a person can't be changed, and those that can take time, whether it's externally stipulated or self-developmentally inspired.

Everyone wants to grow, learn, and better themselves as they can, and herein lies a core obstacle to managers behaving better. They've been taught to invest in themselves and their futures—to idealize "getting ahead"—and the work culture pushes this ideal to an extreme. Managers become so consumed with their own advancement that they lack the capacity to give others the focus they need.

Anxious to accomplish and move ahead, managers become so excessively self-oriented that they treat people working with them, particularly direct reports, as resources to deploy and use in furthering their own success. Assuming this orientation makes it extremely difficult for managers to use what life experience has been trying to teach them—how to get along and enjoy working with imperfect people who think differently than they would like them to think. Too many managers just don't get it. They refuse to accept that imperfect people—people who think and reason differently—are all they're ever going to encounter.

The result is generation after generation of managers possessing unrealistic expectations due to their inability to get human nature straight. To be fair, I don't see managers as entirely responsible for their own bad behavior. Why? Because no one calls them on it. Fathom this. Some companies spend millions of dollars annually on management development programs. They do this without spending a single dollar to research what those same managers think that company leaders expect from them. And yet, it is those very expectations that lead to the employee-alienating survival mechanisms that the management training is aimed at getting them to stop. I'll be telling you about several such mechanisms when I get down to specifics.

So why aren't more employees demanding better treatment? Why do most complain and see bad management as a systemic problem only after some managerial action, or inaction, thwarts their number-one goal: accomplishing what the company needs done and, by doing so, moving their careers ahead. When something particularly negative strikes, coworkers may lend a sympathetic ear, and perhaps even make a few suggestions. But in the end, it's not their problem, and it's not their goals being affected. With little at stake, others limit their involvement. Working in a high-threat environment, they act to safeguard their ambitions as bad management behavior continues, story after story.

While every bad management experience is different, there are some similar themes. One familiar theme has employees being told the mistreatment they're experiencing is actually evidence of good management. For example, consider this account that a company president shared with me. It describes an early-career encounter with a manager that continues to haunt him today. Granted, it's an extreme situation, and most bad management instances are a bit more subtle. But do read it, and when you finish, ask yourself how many similar stories you have heard—and over how many years?

My interview with this vice president did not go well, to say the least. His questions caused me to struggle and stammer. I wanted a change in assignment, but it was an awful interview and, ironically, I was qualified.

Toward the end of the hour he looked at my résumé, noting that it stated I'm an avid food and wine enthusiast. He excused himself for a minute and returned with two Styrofoam cups—one with water and the other with soda. He then asked me to drink from each. After taking a sip, he asked if either cup had wine in it, to which I replied, "No." He responded saying, "Well, at least you know something about wine because you know nothing about finance." I was shocked and found his feedback immensely cruel. Nobody in the entirety of my life ever said anything so spiteful and offensive to me.

Not only did he share his impressions with my direct supervisor and my then division head, he went on to tell them he would have never interviewed me if it wasn't for the relationship my division head had with his boss— the managing director. I was devastated and offended. But most of all, I was distraught that I let my supervisor and division head down.

This isn't the first time I've shared this story, but it's the first time I've realized how profoundly impacted I was by this VP's comments. I was always confident and talkative, but for ten years now I've gone through periods of fearing I'd say the wrong thing at the wrong time, not be articulate when I need to be, and let people down who believe in me. Stupid as it sounds, I've finally come to realize this VP has become a nagging thorn in my side.

I never want to be spoken to or thought about this way again. I never again want to be the object of such spite, judgment, and disappointment. My fear has led to my focusing so much on saying the right thing that my authentic voice becomes garbled. It's come to the point where I find myself saying things entirely different from how I want my message to come across. I hope that by finally recognizing how profoundly this event affected me I'll be my true self again.

Don't get me wrong. Not every manager has a mean streak like the individual dishing out hurt in this story. However unconscionable his behavior seems, I doubt he thinks he has a mean streak. Considering himself a good manager, he probably thought, *It's time someone wises this young guy up for his own and the company's good.*

But, as you will see depicted throughout this book, every manager has been culturally touched to the extent that hurt-causing acts like this become possible, even excusable. Do you think others hearing about its occurrence complained, or put the dishing-it-out manager in his place? I don't. We're living in a work culture that lulls employees into complacency— thinking it's just a few bad managers, or a company in the wrong hands, creating a toxic environment. The thinking goes that once a bad-behaving manager gets his or her next assignment someone more sensitive will come along. People don't realize bad managerial behavior is the consequence of a system that permits it and, yes, causes managers to behave badly without realizing the negatives their behavior inflicts on others.

Sleeper Cells

You want another example of how people slough off bad management behavior? Take Carly Fiorina, the AT&T executive who moved on to head Hewlett-Packard. She's a graduate of more than one esteemed university and no doubt used plenty of good judgment to work her way up in the engineering world. But the quality of Fiorina's judgment began to slip once she became chief executive officer (CEO) of Hewlett-Packard. Her clandestine eavesdropping on the board of directors was cited in a book, written by leadership experts, that portrays sound judgment as the essence of good leadership. The book used her actions to illustrate what falling far short of the gold standard actually looks like.[10]

So why did she do it? Why did she feel the need to use stealth once she rose to the top tier of management? To my way of seeing it, Fiorina had a few blind spots, as all people do. Those blind spots went undetected until she encountered a situation that, in her mind, made dishonest spying acceptable.

While board members at Hewlett-Packard didn't forget or forgive her, most of the world moved on. Her highly publicized "naughty" did not deter communications giant AT&T from inviting her back and making her a member of their board. Nor were more than four million Californians deterred from voting for her in 2010 when she unsuccessfully ran for a seat in the US Senate. Apparently, a lot of people thought her misbehavior was isolated to the work world and wouldn't reoccur in public office.

I see Carly Fiorina's misbehavior as a mere symptom of a problem much larger than her myopia. As I stated, I'm not talking about a few inept managers performing badly, or the kind of sporadic mindlessness into which anyone can lapse. I'm talking about a perverted way of thinking about one's self, and other people, that makes bad management predictable and prevalent in almost every large organization and company, and plenty of smaller ones as well. It's not just some executive drowning in ignominy by having their bad behavior publicly exposed. The problem is far more pervasive than that. It's a sleeper-cell mindset created by blind spots and ambition that, once awakened, can lead almost any manager to malfunction. It's endemic to the way people in management positions have been conditioned to think. It emanates from a perspective that's very flawed.

What I have to say in this book is disturbing. It will especially challenge managers who like to believe that nothing systemically pernicious is taking place. This is a common reaction, and one that reflects how the American work culture socializes people to stick with the positive. But such optimism has its limitations. For one thing, it pushes managers to cherry pick their problems and avoid issues they're not confident they can resolve. Playing it safe, they stick with what the mainstream culture deems correct. They fear being seen doing anything wrong or performing inadequately, and gravitate to treating symptoms instead of grappling with the problems causing those symptoms.

It's like the proverbial drunk looking for lost keys under the lamppost where he has enough light to see instead of the spot where he dropped his keys.

Symptom Relief Doesn't Get Us Relief

I don't see a quick fix for the bad management problems I shine light on in this book. The solution requires expanded consciousness leading to a serious change in managerial focus. It entails living with broken situations that, at least in the near term, most company leaders lack the will to repair. No fix is possible until more people—leaders, managers, operatives, and employees—accurately see what's going on. Getting clarity entails stripping away veneer to expose the pressure points and hidden forces that prevent good management from taking place. That's what I'm out to reveal. I want you to see the force field clearly enough to appreciate what's needed, and know enough about it to involve yourself in changing what, for so long, has been the workplace status quo.

When laying out these misconceptions for managers, there's a refrain from an old tune that I often hear. It's a common refrain that, no matter who's crooning, always sounds off-key to me. It usually starts, "Really, Sam, it's not that bad. Employees can always come to me with their problems. They know that." Oh, do they? How can some managers be so naïve! Do they really think that all it takes is an open-door policy, and an earnest appeal, for employees to feel sufficiently comfortable to speak candidly to people holding the power to determine their fates?

If you need examples of people who paled in the face of power, think about the scores of engineers who didn't speak up about the defect-hiding conspiracy at General Motors (GM), the hundreds of administrators at the Veterans Health Administration who were aware of double bookkeeping appointment–ledgers, and officials and managers at the Port Authority of New York and New Jersey who knew shutting down access lanes to the George Washington Bridge was life-interrupting needless. The open-door policy clearly didn't help in those instances.[11] People knew but didn't speak up for fear of jeopardizing their careers. Who needs more evidence that major differences exist between the words managers speak and the messages their employees receive? I remind managers all the time, "If you want to know what you said, ask people what they heard, and, better yet, look at what they did after you spoke your words."

This raises an important question: What is it about the work culture that has people in management positions thinking that doing right for themselves is more important than doing right for their employees? In management schools we teach students that doing right for employees equates to doing right for oneself. Yet stronger forces undermine this lesson. Most managers claim to be well-intentioned, and appear genuinely disappointed when their actions aren't seen that way. In their minds the gap is caused by the unintended consequences of being overloaded by doing what the job *objectively* requires. And, on the surface, they probably have good reason for thinking this. But digging deeper, I see managers more overloaded by work-culture-provoked insecurities that prevent them from following their good instincts. If good intentions were enough to make good behavior, the workplace would already be transformed.

My Agenda

I intend this book to serve as a splash of cold water in the face for its description of the perverse forces bearing on managers at every level. There are few mysteries about what people want in the way of good managerial behavior. The big mystery has to do with why people aren't receiving what almost everyone, managers included, believe people should receive. Yes, there are many managers doing things right. But relative to the numbers, they're the exception. And by no means is having a good-behaving manager today sufficient reason to believe the next one you get will be the same. The system that socializes and rewards managers prevents it.

Without the system changing, companies will continue implementing piecemeal remedies each time a bad management practice gets revealed. But such solutions only act like mallets used in the Whac-a-Mole games found at carnivals. Each dysfunctional practice that pops up gets whacked with a remedy, only to have another dysfunctional practice pop up. I now see managers tackling one problem and then going on to another, a waste of company resources. It's time to fix the system that keeps the stream of bad management problems coming.

As you read this book, you'll have many opportunities to check its accuracy. You can do so by reflecting on what you've already experienced to see if what's been related helps you to understand more. I'll be revealing hidden aspects of the force field in which the managers, whose bad behavior impacts you, are destined to operate. I'll be making you aware of the reasons that underlie the detrimental behaviors taking place— behaviors you may have missed noticing. Making you aware of what transpires is necessary in order for you to utilize advice I eventually offer. While a good deal of that advice is implied in my narrative going along, I wait until later chapters to get explicit about the actions leaders, managers, and employees who want to stop the flow of bad behavior need to take. I believe the narratives leading up to this advice are essential in order to avoid people inappropriately blaming higher-ups and subsequently misfiring.

I intend to increase your awareness of the bad management behavior you're witnessing, and of why the managers dispensing it are so oblivious to their impact on the people they're out to help. I also want to make you aware of what blocks people who experience bad management behavior from urging company leaders to put a stop to it. While critical about what I see taking place, my purpose is not to admonish and blame; it's to make everyone more aware of what prevents people from getting what they need, and what constructively might be done about it. And I have suggestions.

I expect many readers will feel the urge to talk with others about the realizations they have as they go along. I fully understand this, and believe it a splendid idea—that is, eventually. But I urge restraint. Wait until you finish the last chapter, where I provide some cautionary guidance for discussing what you'd like to see changed. I fear that until you get the entire picture, your insights may alienate some of the people whose indignation you're out to arouse. Eventually you'll need their support and want their camaraderie, and I've got advice for how to proceed when soliciting it.

I find that people who feel they're succeeding prefer the devil they know to the practices they've yet to try. When you think about it, this reasoning makes a lot of sense. Why remove a prop that could destabilize what one fought so long and hard to achieve? Besides, who wants to face the embarrassment of realizing that some *good* management behavior taken was mostly good for oneself, not nearly so good for others, and that the schism was obvious from the start? Talking system change, it's inevitable you'll get pushback. Prepare to deal with it. Think of the resistance you get as a sign that you're on to something. Like Frederick Douglass, the famous American abolitionist, once wrote, "If there is no struggle, there is no progress."

Yes, It's Personal

During a career spent working as an MBA school professor and researcher, I've investigated and exposed many questionable management practices—acquiring a reputation as a muckraker for doing so. Wizened and impatient, I now find myself needing to strike out at the heart of the octopus that, up till now, I've been battling one tentacle at a time. This time, I'm out to expose the so-called *good management* reasoning that leads to bad practices in the first place, and the doublethink reasoning managers use to hide the negatives their actions effect—from employees, from cohort managers, and, I hate saying this, especially from themselves. Until this reasoning and the circumstances responsible for it are denounced, I fear that bad management will continue as the norm.

It's time for managers to face some missing facts, and to rethink what they call good management. I believe greater awareness of the forces corrupting their behavior, and a more solid connection with their humanity, is the route to managers realizing their good intentions. I see the heart of good management grounded in human nature facts. That is, *real* human nature facts, not the warped versions some managers like to concoct when trying to convince themselves they understand people.

This is where we begin.

Notes

1. This is an often cited, empirically documented fact. For example, see this study reporting findings from over 10,000 companies for a decade: N. Bloom, C. Genakos, R. Sadun, and J. Van Reenen, "Management Practices across Firms and Countries," *Academy of Management Perspectives* 26, no. 1 (2012): 12–33.

2. A poll conducted of visitors to the Monster.com website, reported November 25, 2014, had more than one in three of 2,700-plus respondents rating their boss "horrible," and over half giving their boss a negative rating. http://www.monster. com/about/a/think-your-friends-have-horrible-bosses-too-youre-probably-right

3. An extensive analysis of MBA programs by a celebrated researcher and MBA professor concludes there is no reason to expect performance in school to translate into effective management practice. H. Mintzberg, *Managers Not MBAs: A Hard Look at the Soft Practice of Managing and Management Development* (San Francisco: Berrett-Koehler, 2005).

4. An August 2007 survey by the Institute for Corporate Productivity (i4cp) in conjunction with HR.com found that almost half—about 47 percent—of the 338 organizations surveyed have no training programs for new supervisors. http:// www.amanet.org/training/articles/The-High-Cost-of-the-Bad-Boss.aspx#sthash.9T8QeBQO.dpuf

5. Results from a poll of one thousand US adults in March 2007 by the Employment Law Alliance (ELA) found that "44% of American workers have worked for a supervisor or employer who they consider abusive." See more at http://www.ama-net.org/training/articles/The-High-Cost-of-the-Bad-Boss. aspx#sthash.9T8QeBQO.dpu

6. State of the American Manager, Gallup Company publication, 2015. http://www.gallup.com/services/182138/state-american-manager.aspx

7. A great number of research studies report trust in one's manager and an organization's top management enables a person to better focus on their work and consequently to be more productive. For example, see R.C. Mayer and M.B. Gavin, "Trust in Management and Performance: Who Minds the Shop While Employees Watch the Boss?" *Academy of Management Journal* 48, no. 5 (2005): 874–88.

8. S.J. Schroeder, "An Investigation into the Psychology of Individuals' Empowerment at Work" (dissertation, UCLA's Anderson School of Management, 1998).

9. There are several studies reporting that people who experience abusive situations at work also report more work-caused distress in the family life. For an example, see B.J. Tepper, "Consequences of Abusive Supervision," *Academy of Management Journal* 43, no. 2 (2000): 178–90.

10. W.G. Bennis and N. Nichey, *Judgment: How Winning Leaders Make Great Calls* (New York: Penguin, 2007).

11. Attesting to this reluctance is a study where 85 percent of participants indicated having been in situations where they felt uncomfortable raising important issues with a supervisor. F.J. Milliken, E.W. Morrison, and P.F. Hewlin, "An Exploratory Study of Employee Silence: Issues that Employees Don't Communicate Upward and Why," *Journal of Management Studies* 40, no. 6 (2003): 1,453–76.

2

DOUBLETHINK

HOW MANAGERS CONVINCE
THEMSELVES BAD BEHAVIOR
IS GOOD MANAGING

This isn't the first time culture has warped good intentions, preventing people from doing what they know is right. American history is full of examples. Think about the slave trade and people living in the Jim Crow South. Plenty of well-meaning people knew slavery and institutionalized racism were atrocious, but the thought of change was overwhelming. Instead of following their conscience, they went along with this way of life with the hope of coming out on top.

Take Thomas Jefferson, author of the Declaration of Independence, for example. Historians say he was morally against slavery, but he still bought into the system, with nearly two hundred slaves to his name.[1,2] He could have used his political might to speak out, but Jefferson instead found ways to rationalize his consent and support for this immoral practice. Like many others, he overrode his sensibilities to go along with a culture-endorsed system that enabled him to live a privileged life.

I find a troubling parallel in today's workplace. There are too many well-meaning people who know better, who override their sensibilities and play along with what they see the mainstream culture rewarding, hoping to realize their goals for success. They play mind games, trying to believe that there's no better way to manage people, or interact with them, without jeopardizing their own aspirations and success. In the end it's all about keeping your job, getting ahead, and ignoring the costs.

I see a large part of this mentality embedded in the narrative with which people grew up. Nearly every grade-school social studies class gives lessons on how Americans are independent, goal-focused, and relentlessly determined to improve their prospects in life. Our textbook heroes had humble beginnings. They overcame insurmountable obstacles. They accomplished more than anyone dreamt was possible—so the stories go. Davy Crockett, Jackie Robinson, even Oprah Winfrey—they're the stuff of legends. These hardworking, talented people demonstrate that, with enough grit and determination, all things are possible. That's the American way; it's the bedrock work ethic.

Managing the American Way

The world of management personifies this perfectly. It's where people get noticed for their individual accomplishments and promoted for long hours and steadfast determination. The culture is about learning essentials, sticking to your guns, building image, climbing the ranks, and using cunning and stature to intimidate those in your way. Donald Trump spoke candidly about this: "My style of doing things is fairly simple. I just push, push, and push again what I want to achieve."[3] However irritating he might be, Donald was honest about his approach. Most managers I know are more subdued in owning up to self-interested agendas, but they operate the same way as Mr. Trump. Pushing to get ahead is the name of the game in today's work culture.

But here's the thing—that's not "management." Whether they realize it or not, managers have been conditioned to follow a culturally inspired script that's obsessed with self-success. However, in their zeal to succeed, managers over-look their number one assignment—setting the stage, and cre-ating the conditions, for *others* to accomplish and, yes, succeed. I've worked with and coached managers for decades, and it's rare to hear one admit to dereliction of this assignment. Their intentions are in the right place, and they think they're doing a good job for their direct reports. But truth be told—and it's a hard truth to swallow—their focus is on staging the condi-tions for their own success, not the success of their reports.

It's like a Boy Scout out to do a good deed trying to help an old lady cross the street in a direction she doesn't want to go. Confused by the old lady's resistance, the scout never thinks to ask where she's headed. He's out to earn the Good Samaritan badge and can't imagine his interests not aligning with those of the lady he's ostensibly out to help.

In the same way, most managers never think to ask their employees this simple question: "What do you need from me, and how can I help you?" Rather, they announce the direc-tion in which they're headed and just assume "the team" will follow. Then they're puzzled when direct reports don't show equal enthusiasm. When they encounter inertia, their backup tactic is like Mr. Trump's "push again." Of course, the direc-tion they've chosen has something in it for them; if it didn't, they would be proceeding differently. In their minds, it's the employees who don't get it. Then again, maybe the inertia employees show signals it's the managers who don't get it.

Don't get me wrong: managers owe it to themselves to accomplish and advance. But they also owe direct reports the guidance and support required for them to do the same. When someone's job title includes the word *manager* and direct reports are involved, the core motive should not be self-success attained by leading the way and taking credit for what the team accomplishes. Instead, good management behavior requires stepping back from the limelight and putting self-pursuits on hold. It's about helping direct reports to merge what's unique and important to them with the needs of the enterprise employing them. That is good management in the true sense of the word.

I'm disheartened to find this perspective so often absent in the minds of people with management titles. Asked to describe the functions of a good manager, they all give at least lip service to an "other-directed" focus. It's the politically correct response. But when push comes to shove, even the most empathetic and well-intentioned people seem unable to set self-interest aside. Despite everything written about the supportive role managers should play,[4] it's not the American way for managers to make others' success their primary objective at the risk of neglecting their own. In fact, managers who subordinate their needs to help employees can appear coddling, and even a bit wimpy, in the eyes of their peers.

A Rising Tide Lifts All Boats

Like Donald Trump, most managers like to insist that things be done as they want them done. That's why it's so common to see direct reports deployed as operatives in accomplishing results that accrue to their manager. If I challenge bosses on this, as I sometimes do, most cite the urgency of company-needed results as the reason for steering employees down a path to success—as defined and orchestrated by that manager, of course. Since the managers charted and blazed the trail their operatives traversed, they get the major credit for what those operatives accomplished. No question about it, lots of people with manager titles know how to lead and direct. It's just that the people working for them think of themselves as more than operatives and do-what-you're-told functionaries. Strange how people with egos and distinctive identities like to be seen. They don't want to be seen as interchangeable; they don't want to be someone's widget.

Self-justifying the directive role they play, many managers invoke some variation of the "a rising tide lifts all boats" aphorism. If the manager's vision works, then everyone benefits, or so their thinking goes. Even though only a few managers brag—it's not considered good form—all keep a list of accomplishments to recite when their bonus and salary are discussed. Who blames them? The whole work culture is about accomplishing, credit-taking, individual recognition, and getting ahead. If this is true for employees, it's especially true for managers. It's the American tradition; it's how the world of work breathes and lives.

But deep down, something doesn't feel right about this. Managers know they can't just come out and say everything they've done was for themselves. They'd lose credibility and respect, not to mention the trust of direct reports. Of course, well-meaning managers don't realize that this is what they've been doing all along. After all, keeping a tally of accomplishments is ingrained in the system. It takes a good deal of reflection and uncomfortable honesty for people to grasp their real intentions.

Most managers recognize the importance of covering over their credit-taking with humility—at least with their direct reports. Disingenuously, they thank "the hardworking people on the team who performed the work." But the "team" doesn't get the bonus, promotion, or management stature. Sometimes there's a symbolic cash award or an employee-of-the-month photo on the cafeteria wall. Seldom does something material and lasting trickle down to operatives. The manager gets the credit and the bigger paycheck that goes with it. Whose boat rose with the tide after all?

Needless to say, this kind of self-serving management style doesn't fly with employees. They don't like managers claiming that every directive, guideline, and stipulation they gave was intended to benefit the team. Even the most naïve employee eventually sees such claims as inauthentic and begins to feel used. I've seen too many employees become completely deflated after realizing their hard work resulted in a promotion or bonus—not for themselves but for their boss. This is no way to motivate a team to give their all. Outside of people who work on idealistic causes, such as political campaigns and humanitarian efforts, employees don't put in long hours merely to advance their boss's ambitions. They expect something out of it too. But many managers never get that straight.

Consumed with self-advancing pursuits, managers don't recognize their own ongoing failure to provide something essential direct reports need: an other-directed focus. Ironically, that other-directed focus is the very thing that, in another moment, managers fault their own bosses for not providing them. That's right, when acting as direct reports, managers "get it." They know what's missing because it's what they want for themselves. They know good management means creating the conditions for direct reports to succeed in the ways they envisioned when they took their job and assumed their assignments. But when acting as managers, these same people appear clueless. One might think of what managers fail to get from their bosses as poetic justice served.

Meanwhile, top-tier managers are on the hook for overall jurisdiction results. They need to get the best possible performance out of everyone so the company can grow and prosper—which is in everybody's interests. That's why the term *manager* was invented. I'm not talking about managers simply driving employees to get more accomplished. Darth Vader can run a tight ship, but who would want to work for him? I'm talking about managers taking an other-directed focus by learning enough about each report to contour assignments in ways that allow them to achieve and progress on their individually held goals. People arrive to the job motivated. The real trick is to avoid turning them off.

Who Gets the Blame?

Think of it this way. Imagine a parent who wants the very best for their children. They want to help their children discover what they love to do, and find ways to pursue it. In a similar way, managerial work is about developing an authentic concern for each direct report. This means learning enough to appreciate each employee's unique capacities, and knowing where that individual wants to go. Then, just like a good parent, a good manager sets the stage for employees to realize their full potential, and succeed as they themselves, not their managers, envision. I'm talking about a manager practicing "mindset management,"[5] not insisting reports live in their "US of Me."

Did you notice what's distinct in how I'm portraying the management function? I didn't describe good management practiced through command-and-control, hierarchical relationships, where the employee is the only one held accountable. I'm portraying a *reciprocally* accountable relationship where each person is committed to helping the other accomplish what the company needs in ways that are unique and meaningful to the person performing the activity. The employee is responsible for accomplishing company-needed results, and the manager is responsible for ensuring that the company gets what it needs by establishing the conditions required for the employee to be and contribute their best.[6]

I find it absurd when a manager gets rewarded while one or more direct reports fail to deliver company-needed results. It's absurd because the manager also dropped the ball. The way I see it, the manager's job is to provide each employee the support, coaching, oversight, and help that allows that employee to achieve results the best way the employee knows how. Defining it this way, a manager fails the company each time one of their reports fails to deliver.

Sure, not everyone's able to succeed at each task assigned them. That's because employees come with limitations, just like managers do. There are always grounds for grading an employee down and holding them accountable for mistakes made, and for what they failed to deliver. But, to be fair, the grading should account for the fact that the employee had a manager who selected them for a task they couldn't perform, and then failed to provide the additional resources the employee needed to get the job done.

The bottom line is that managers should take the time to really get to know their employees. Without understanding the abilities and limitations of the people reporting to them, managers won't know what personal imperfections to work around so they don't sink end results. When a disappointing performance occurs, the manager shouldn't get off scot-free. The company counts on everyone to do their jobs to the best of their ability, including the bosses. I've had to speak up for companies and remind managers of this. I tell them, "Up until the time either you or your report moves on, your job is to get the very best that the individual has to give the company. Period."

The way I see things, both parties have skin in the game. Neither succeeds when the other doesn't. I like it when managers and direct reports discuss how things are going, flag trouble spots for one another, and realistically discuss who has the skills and time to do what. I especially like it when managers check in with their reports, inquiring if there's anything more that they need. I like it even more when reports feel comfortable enough to answer truthfully. It's about being proactive rather than reactive. But managers consumed in self-interested pursuits often lack the time and inclination to ask questions, let alone learn the reasons for the difficulties an employee has. Even when they do have time, managers too seldom take an other-directed focus that includes learning the strengths and limitations, interests, and aspirations of their reports.

Lacking such a focus, employees get lumped into categories, and too much is assumed. The worst example is how top-tier managers blithely assume employees will warn them when something's amiss. In chapter 1, I wrote about General Motors and the Veterans Health Administration managers learning this lesson the hard way—that is, if they actually learned it. That same year, even the prized Secret Service suffered a slew of institutional comeuppances. Entire administrations would not have come under fire if employees had felt comfortable raising issues with their managers, and if mid-level managers felt comfortable doing the same with their higher-ups. But clearly, the right people didn't feel comfortable enough. Despite federal legislation that protects whistle-blowers, people in the know found it self-advantageous to remain quiet.

The Boy Scout's Coping Mechanism

I can't count the number of managers who, in confidence, have shared something they felt to be grossly wrong about how people in their company were being managed. Citing one mandated practice or another, or some out-of-control cohort manager wreaking havoc, they acknowledge systemic obstacles to employee effectiveness. But few speak up about what's wrong, or about the remedy implied by the problem statement they formulate. And those who do feel obligated to attempt a fix generally do just enough to assuage employees, while avoiding saying or doing anything that might rankle a cohort manger or a person higher up. Why do managers act as if their hands are tied when it comes to fixing things for direct reports? Why are they so concerned about rankling a peer? Whatever the reason, it doesn't get publicly discussed.

Herein lie several conundrums managers aren't able to reconcile. Combined, they account for bad management behavior being more norm than exception. If a manager's core responsibility is setting the stage for direct reports to perform their best, why are managers with failing reports considered successful and deserving of more responsibility? Why are managers not called derelict for failing to notice, remove, and replace practices and protocols that systemically block the effective functioning of people they are mandated to assist? And, how do managers fool themselves into believing they're practicing good management behavior when the people reporting to them are afraid to tell them what's actually on their minds? Wouldn't you think managers might lose image and credibility admitting to conundrums like these? Apparently they would, which explains why so few acknowledge them.

This is where doublethink enters the picture. Doublethink is the coping mechanism managers use to explain away the negative outcomes their actions, and inaction, hold for others on the grounds they were doing what the work culture stipulates good managers are supposed to do. It's the rationale that allows managers to justify just about anything they do— regardless of the negatives inflicted. Doublethink allows managers to override their sensibilities, and to mute the inner voice that tells them they should be doing more for their reports. It's the "rising tide lifts all ships" rationalization for not performing the most essential part of their managerial function— making it possible for others to accomplish, develop, and succeed on grounds important to those others.

Of course, no well-intentioned manager wants to see themself relying on doublethink to manage. No manager owning up to using doublethink could see themself doing a good managerial job. They might think themselves self-serving, manipulative, duplicitous, or who knows what else.

Don't Rock the Boat

Think again about our well-intentioned Boy Scout. Just like many upwardly striving managers, his compass is set to accumulating merit badges, not to helping the old lady get where she wants to go. And, in this instance, he's got his eye on promotion to Eagle Scout. Talk about a one-track mind focused on personal accomplishment! If you could ask him, you'd probably learn he honestly thinks he's performing good deeds for others. Now this scout is off to earn his "Good Manager" badge. Given his role models, I'm afraid to imagine what he's got up his sleeve for that one.

Most managers aren't as clueless as our well-meaning Boy Scout. Many have their own lists of grievances, and see dysfunction at higher levels as the cause. They complain that their organization's policies and practices make it hard to give managing their all, to engage in selfless acts, and to speak their truths, and still receive the recognition and promotions due them. These managers tell me how upsetting it is when they see their own bosses fabricate truth and insist on practices that promote distrust within the ranks. So naturally I ask what they've done to fix what they see as broken. That question elicits a list of "the system won't let me" explanations nearly as long as their list of grievances.

Managers convincingly tell me it's not their role, speaking up won't get them anywhere, and, besides, it's not smart to be seen rocking the boat. They mention their fear of alienating cohort managers who appear content with the status quo. They tell me that they're doing a good job turning out results and helping employees, all considered. So, one minute they complain about bad management above them. Then the next minute, when the ball is placed in their court, they immediately switch tunes and, helped by doublethink, drift into saying, "Well, it's not so bad after all."

It gets better though. What shocks me next is how these same managers think that they're doing a good enough job by not changing anything. They have the nerve to call their reluctance "effective managerial action." No, this is the opposite of effective managerial action; it's *ineffectiveness* through managerial *inaction*.

Their response never sits well with the people reporting to them who find their daily effectiveness constrained. It doesn't sit well with me, even though I see them hemmed in by forces of which they are unaware. And it doesn't even sit well with them. Doublethink comes with a cost for everyone, especially the companies counting on allegedly world-class managers to get the best from everyone employed. Most people want to give it their all, and deserve better than mystifying managerial statements. There are actions that can be taken. Managers fool themselves by pretending there aren't. Stephen Hawking said it very well: "I have noticed even people who claim everything is predestined, and that we can do nothing to change it, look before they cross the road."[7]

Doublethink's Paralysis

The thing is, change is always possible, no matter how much people convince themselves otherwise. Culture is not an entity that stands on its own. Ask any sociologist or anthropologist. They'll tell you that culture is a social construction. That means people create it and people can change it. You'd think people's tolerance for doublethink excuses would be wearing thin; I know mine is. I'm tired of listening to top-level managers saying it's too difficult to sell the idea of change to other managers whose endorsements are needed for a company-wide fix.

You want an example? Listen to what this lead engineer working in aerospace thinks about management's reluctance to change one obvious and simple thing. It's a fix that would greatly benefit the company, yet everybody's afraid to make a move. See if any of this sounds familiar.

Along with others in aerospace and defense, our company is facing a wave of upcoming retirements. I am deeply perplexed by the poor job we are doing replacing critical subject-matter experts. I see a total absence in training due, in large part, to our complicated management system.

In short, the company is "matrix managed," meaning the typical employee has two mutually exclusive management chains—one for their function (i.e., software engineering) and one for their product-line business area (i.e., satellite communications). And, it's generally agreed that each function is 'responsible' for training people to perform their function's work. When there are program-level reviews that include management from both sides of the matrix, people don't know how to respond to questions like, "What is going to happen when Rick, the software engineer working in satellites, retires?" Quickly, everyone looks to the line manager responsible for software engineering for some kind of answer. You can count on him to nod his head as if he plans on doing something. And he follows script. No one from either side of the management matrix claims responsibility for preparing someone to replace Rick.

I've seen several examples of this over the last two months as we close in on retirements that we're totally unprepared to handle. I've heard explanations listing what has been done and what still has to happen, but it's really all bullshit. And I know it's bullshit because the software-engineering organization lacks a budget for training. Even if someone wanted to train replacements like they pretend they do, they can't!

I'm stunned thinking how so many smart managers can sit by, watching a pending disaster unfold without pointing out the obvious: functional organizations like ours have no resources for addressing the looming problem in front of them. All their nodding agreement doesn't mean a thing. When the stuff hits the fan no one's going to remember there was no training budget to begin with. They're all going to play dumb and deny any accountability. Every person questioned will merely say, "I fully intended to have replacements trained, but any training becomes a cost-overrun that could negatively affect our getting future business.' Since everyone's guilty of the same offense, no one is going to point a finger, and no one is going to take a hit."

Okay, let me ask those familiar with management in large companies: Did anything in this example surprise you? Do you call this good management? Do you think what's happening in this company is different from what's happening in other companies, or other industries? I'll bet that none of your answers were in the affirmative.

As usually happens in mismanaged situations, it's the company that stands to lose the most. In instances like this, you have managers acting as if they're hostages to one another's doublethink. They behave as if they're afraid to get involved.

Instead of rolling up their sleeves and working to remove bureaucratic obstacles, they leave it to their direct reports to come up with a solution. In a short time they'll be talking like Monday morning quarterbacks making "should have done this" statements to sidestep accountability for their stalled operation. They'll take some heat for their inaction, but not nearly as much as they must have fantasized thinking about how, with no cross-charging, training replacements would make their numbers look bad. I would hardly call their failure to get involved and take responsibility for getting replacements trained effective managerial action.

I imagine that the aerospace engineers, rather than their managers, will ultimately be blamed for this breakdown—at least that's how hard-to-identify-who-was-responsible derelictions like this usually go down. Regrettably, I find very few managers willing to realize that a struggling employee's poor performance is the result of actions they refused to take. Employees make easy scapegoats. All it takes is a bit of doublethink.

Don't get me wrong: not all managers blow off their responsibilities. Conversations with bosses have convinced me that most retain the capacity to recognize what should take place— that is, when the individual needing to act differently is someone else. But when their own inaction is questioned, it's easy for a manager just to evade. As the aerospace staffing problem clearly illustrates, all one needs to do is nod.

Thanks to hierarchy, managers don't have to answer to employees. And when they do, it's seldom more than a lip-service acknowledgement such as, "Thanks for bringing it up. That's really important. I'll take it under advisement." They say this knowing full well that bosses above them will never hear. And when the consequences become too noticeable to overlook, some managers will go so far as to impose additional top-down controls and procedural policing. They'll justify the need for added employee surveillance by citing a situation created by their unwillingness to fix a broken system. Talk about doublethink!

"Why Didn't You Say Something?"

At this point, the scenario is staged for the coup de grâce of doublethink, and some managers just can't resist. Scrambling to save face and maintain credibility with direct reports, they agree that some things need to change but then argue, "We can't do it now." Why not now? Because other managers, certainly not themselves, lack sufficient skills to manage without the top-down controls afforded by the bad management practices they just joined employees in criticizing. In their minds, they're doing their peers a good service. They rationalize that truth-spinning and blame-dodging are necessary to help less adequate managers maintain the trust and respect of their reports.

Hello? Hello? Is anybody listening? That's right—the doublethink reasoning managers give to justify *lying* to employees is helping peers maintain their employees' *trust*.

To make matters worse, few managers understand that hierarchy should be kept out of relationships. And those who do seldom know how. Hierarchy is good for structure but it's toxic in a relationship. Its presence puts employees on the defensive, disinclined to ask managers for the support and resources they need. Employees believe revealing the problems they're having with their managers will get them scored deficient. In fact, most employees believe that mentioning any need for managerial assistance they're not receiving, especially help with a performance difficulty, invites criticism, not managerial support. They fear their unmet needs will be heard as complaints that will linger in their manager's mind, and later reconciled by their being graded down.

So we're left with managers telling employees that they need to voice their concerns, but failing to provide the safeguards employees need to speak freely and push back when their manager interrupts. And who's at fault? You know the answer. Employees are blamed for not speaking up.

Here's a vivid example of an employee learning *not* to speak up. I believe I could collect literally a thousand examples similar to this.

> The CEO tells me to put together a proposal where we offer our client an advertising platform at twice their budget, and using approaches that will never get them what they need. I find myself unable to tell him everything he's proposing is 100 percent wrong. In past encounters, I've been ignored when I voiced any dissent on matters about which I was hired to be the company expert. He makes me feel like I'm a soldier disobeying orders. So in this situation, I gently voice my opposition, and then tell him I will do whatever he feels is best for the client team and our organization. Deliberately, I withhold expressing how strongly I believe the approach he's taking betrays the trust we've developed with the client— that led to our getting their business. Feeling once again ignored, I can tell you that this is the last time, until the day I can get myself a job somewhere else, that I will ever say anything sounding like a contrary opinion.

This narrative illustrates the negatives of what I call *hierarchical command and control power-taking*. A frustrated employee concludes that he has far more to gain by pleasing his boss than speaking up about what he believes to be best practices for the company. And who will pay the price? The client and, ultimately, the people who invested in this company, once the client decides to move on. Albeit on a less consequential scale, I see this employee's situation paralleling what Veterans Health administrators and GM engineers went through when contemplating their whistle-blowing options. Fearful of speaking up, their silence cost patients and drivers their lives.

I find that any time hierarchy enters a work relationship you can count on employees becoming intimidated. Not only do employees fear sticking up for the company's interests, they fear sticking up for themselves. They dread the consequences of telling their manager what they actually think and feel, such as, "Here's what I need changed in your thinking and managerial approach in order to work the best way I know how." Getting the obedience and acquiescence they like, few managers notice the kowtowing they receive. In fact, most managers fail to notice anything wrong with a hierarchical system that allows them to hold employees accountable for just about anything they decide to criticize or insist on.

I see a manager's satisfaction with one-sided accountability as clear-cut evidence of a manager not assuming responsibility for ensuring the effectiveness of their direct reports. They don't see the "damned if they do, damned if they don't" predicament that garbles employees' voices. The only way for employees to document what they need their manager to change in their dealings with them is to admit to not being able to do their jobs very well. Appropriately, I think, they fear providing managers the grounds for labeling the ineffectiveness they reference the result of employee ineptitude, not mismanagement. Thanks to doublethink, that's easy to do. So the cycle of misunderstanding goes on, and on, and on.

Real Accountability Is Two-Sided

Okay, you get the picture. Managers are human beings, needy, imperfect, and with image needs just like the rest of us. With one-sided accountability and doublethink as props, it's unrealistic to expect them to take stock of mistakes and shortcomings, use of duplicity, and camouflaged dereliction. But there's a cost of which they're unaware. The more doublethink managers use, the more illogic and duplicity they expose to people who, at a future time, might find it advantageous to debunk them. It's a vulnerability that builds with time.

I find very few managers resisting the momentary conveniences afforded by one-sided accountability and doublethink. The best way I've found to inhibit their usage is to eliminate the motive for people to deceive one another. This is done by revamping managerial relationships to make accountability two-sided. Hold the employee accountable for bringing in results, and hold the manager accountable for the employee's successful performance. Then, no one wins if the other doesn't succeed, and both gain by transparency. When an employee isn't achieving positive results, the support, guidance, and oversight the manager is giving becomes the first variable under the microscope. Provide the manager a reason to earnestly inquire what each employee needs, and employees a no-fault logic for telling them. Put the manager's skin in the game and doublethink becomes a liability. I have much more to say about this, and will as we move forward.

Conclusion

Important questions remain. Why do managers who, after all employee viewpoints are aired, get to make the decision they want, up-play hierarchy to squelch employee voice and input? What allows blatant managerial conundrums to go open-endedly unaddressed? Answers to questions like these get us closer to identifying the core impediment to managers living out their good intentions. Getting answers requires peeling back another layer of the onion to examine how people get chosen for managerial assignments, and the people skills managers acquire while moving up the hierarchy. That's what I want to demystify for you next.

Notes

1. Eric Foner, "The Master and the Mistress," *New York Times*, October 3, 2008. http://www.nytimes.com/2008/10/05/books/review/Foner-t.html?pagewanted=all

2. Paul Finkelman, "The Monster of Monticello," *New York Times*, November 30, 2012. http://www.nytimes.com/2012/12/01/opinion/the-real-thomas-jefferson.html

3. Clever Quotes, StatusMind.com, accessed September 13, 2015. http://statusmind.com/clever-facebook-status-2578/

4. P. Block, *Stewardship* (San Francisco: Berrett-Koehler, 2013); P. Block, *The Empowered Manager* (San Francisco: Jossey-Bass, 1987).

5. This is the term used in a book I authored: *Mind-Set Management: The Heart of Leadership* (New York: Oxford University Press, 1994).

6. S.A. Culbert and J.B. Ullmen, *Don't Kill the Bosses!* (San Francisco: Berrett-Kohler, 2004).

7. S. Hawkins, *Black Holes and Baby Universes and Other Essays* (New York: Bantam, 1993).

3

WHAT PEOPLE SKILLS DO MANAGERS (ACTUALLY) ACQUIRE?

I must have heard a jillion stories explaining why someone was selected for a managerial assignment. Of course, at-hand availability, comfort level, and merit are always mentioned. But digging deeper, I find the selection almost always based on someone's, or some committee's, gut-feel belief that the person selected will get work that needs doing accomplished—reliably, technically, and practically. Take note. I didn't say they were selected for their interpersonal style, emotional intelligence, team-play mentality, or ability to communicate and actively listen. You know, all the skill sets human resource (HR) professionals cite when stipulating what the company needs in a manager.

Keep in mind there are two kinds of managerial jobs: jobs managing functions and jobs managing managers. *Function* refers to an activity that people can see taking place and from which tangible results are expected. Sales is a function; so are engineering, marketing, maintenance, accounting, information technology (IT), and just about every activity that produces an effect one can see. For our purposes now, let's start with how functional managers are selected. That's where the majority of managers begin their climb up the hierarchy. It's also where the formative experiences that determine how managers think about the people they manage take place, and where they eventually learn the people skills required for making it to the next managerial level and beyond.

I find most selectors act on the assumption that, until someone proves otherwise, anyone can be a manager. During the hiring process, many selectors talk core competencies, but seldom included in what they list is interest in, and skills for, working with people. It seems people skills only become a factor after a new manager gets into "trouble." The trouble may be in the form of disappointing work-unit results, or from people complaining about the way they're being managed.

Seldom are one person's complaints called "trouble." One person complaining is usually chalked up to a manager developing "sea legs." No intervention is deemed necessary. I mean, you don't want a new manager distracted, preoccupied with someone scrutinizing every action they take. Good management of managers requires giving people ample opportunity to work out problems for themselves. However, when more than one person complains, it's best to get that manager some "help," so the thinking goes. Better to nip the problem in the bud. Get this person some coaching and training lest their insensitivity negatively impact others, and ultimately company results. In the process, the assumption that anyone can manage goes unexamined.

I realize what I've been describing is different from the storied state-of-the-art selection processes large companies use when recruiting someone to manage a function. Yes, many large companies use recruiters and HR professionals who consider people skills a priority. But after HR vetting, the recruit comes to the company to be interviewed by people whose prime concern is getting work performed competently—whatever it takes. They don't worry about people skills; everybody has them.[1] It's a "get the job covered and train the manager later" mentality.

This is how the fast-talking star salesman gets appointed sales manager. Someone assumed his stand-out results would transfer, perhaps by osmosis, to other sales people. Likewise for the socially reserved, hardworking woman who so competently gets IT work performed. Someone with authority believes too many like activities are being performed differently, and worries that the company is not getting best practices across the board. That individual then concludes it's time to collect individual functionaries and provide them a manager to even out quality and workload. I realize I'm using clichéd examples of situations in which people skills are ignored but, sadly, clichéd thinking like this is today's rule rather than the exception.

You want a specific? Here's one that's right on point. It's excerpted from a paper turned in at the first session of a "Leadership, Motivation & Power" course I teach to fully employed professionals working on their MBAs. Taking care not to bias their responses, I ask students to describe "a personal experience where either good or bad management was apparent." By the way, can you guess what type of management, good or bad, fifty-seven of sixty-two students wrote about? I bet you can, and you're correct! At least five students had a good management experience they could write about. Here's one from the many accounts of bad management:

The worst manager I ever met was me. I was hastily appointed by the senior partner in charge of ABC Investors' New York office. He chose me after two sales guys almost came to blows over who got the commission for a jointly serviced client. The guy I replaced quit when, dealing with the brouhaha, the senior partner stepped in to decide things. Later on, when that partner asked me to step up to manager, I told him I lacked any experience. But I couldn't talk him out of me. He said not to worry. I could count on him to hold my hand.

I was twenty-six, four years out of college, and this was my first job in finance. To say it was learning under fire would be a gross understatement. I lacked interpersonal skills, never managed, but did think I had passion and could motivate. Reporting to me was a large team of twenty sales executives and five traders. Each sales executive had a different background and idiosyncratic goals.

In retrospect, I see how misguided I was spending the majority of my time trying to mold them to fit my vision of what professionals in a Wall Street firm should be. It never occurred to me that I should have been trusting them to find their own style and mission. And the partner who was supposed to co-manage the group, and guide me, treated me like a dog. Our titles were supposed to make us equals, but he hoarded information and created a faux camaraderie that evaporated every time he didn't like what I said.

I find reason for guarded optimism here. Working to get his MBA, this man signed up for an elective that might serve his resolve to make himself a better manager. Look at the sacrifices he makes in trying to improve. He works full-time, studies in the evenings, and goes to school on weekends, not to mention shouldering the expensive tuition. I can't imagine what more a well-intentioned person wanting to learn how to manage might do. But, and this is a big but, it's an open-ended question whether MBA schooling is going to deliver "the goods" he needs for living out his good intentions. After all, the latest statistics[2] show that over one hundred thousand MBAs graduate from US universities annually. That means in less than ten years there'll be a million more MBAs in US companies, with a high percentage holding managerial jobs. This should be the good news but I'm not sure it is. Consider all the MBA graduates up to now. There's no evidence that what is clearly off is getting fixed. What are these people being taught?

Graduate Schools of Success

Given the numbers, it's obvious that part of the problem in getting good management is rooted in what's emphasized in

schools of management. Sorry to say, I don't see much emphasis on providing MBAs the skill sets needed for helping *others*
accomplish and succeed. Sure, some interpersonal skills are
taught, such as "active listening" and "getting to yes" nego-
tiations. But what's needed, and not often enough taught, is
active inquiry, power-sharing, and collaborative skills that
begin with taking stock of one's self. Not many students learn
the importance of straight-talk relationships, and of actually
engaging what other people tell them, especially when it goes
counter to what they want to hear—not as an obstacle to circumvent, but as an opportunity to enhance their perspective
and better relate. Too seldom are students taught to reflect
about how their upbringing affects their worldview, and how
both impact their interactions with people at work. Such reflection is essential in learning to appreciate mindsets and mentalities different from one's own, and in realizing that, more
often than not, the root cause of what one finds off-putting in
others resides in one's own psyche.

But introspective topics like these are glossed over in MBA
schools, if even taught. So when these bright minds enter the
workforce, it's no wonder they don't think to ask questions of
themselves or others. They graduate ready to compete and
dominate rather than interact, respect, and eventually bond
with people who will never think in the same way as they do.

Consider today's MBA schools as an entity, and the role
model they provide. Just like people, they're consumed by the
work culture's extreme focus on success—competing with one
another for rankings and stature. The people running these
schools have also drunk the water and use increases in their
school's stature to document that they are accomplishing. Even
though they're called schools of management, it's clear that the
emphasis is not on management. It's on equipping individuals to succeed. That's how they get students to pay big bucks,
and that's how these schools get their prestige. Many vari-
ables may be used in compiling the rankings, but none is more
important than having graduates recruited into high-stature,

big-paying jobs. If "truth in representing" was upheld, instead of MBA schools being called graduate schools of management, they would be called *graduate schools of success*.

If you don't believe me, check out the courses. I'd venture that over 90 percent of the courses in most MBA schools teach disciplinary skills and economic analysis. Even when the label "organizational behavior" is used in the course description, only a few courses emphasize other-directedness. And students taking those courses literally refer to them as "soft-skill classes." No one recognizes that this is a drastic misnomer, or tries to correct it. But calling them soft skills is correct, at least with respect to the surface-level treatment these topics receive. It's not uncommon for students who get As to go out and flunk the practicum application. They may be able to recite the theory, but seldom do they graduate knowing how to identify what other people are up to, why it's important to them, and how to interact authentically with people reasoning differently than they want them to think and behave. This is a real shame, because it's essential for all managers to have the inclination and the ability to appreciate and value thinking disparate from their own. MBA schools would be a great place to learn to do this, and to practice skills that help them do so.

Sure, MBA students are exposed to the value of making a social contribution, and many get involved performing community service. So there is some sense of other-directedness encouraged in these programs. But the key motivation for student involvement is building a résumé that appeals to recruiters. It's about distinguishing one's self from the pack, and doing whatever good deeds it takes to create a stand-out image.

Teamwork is also emphasized in MBA curriculum, along with learning the importance of harmonizing different work styles. Here is another opportunity to practice understanding why others feel compelled to behave as they do, and the valuing of mindsets different from one's own. But this learning opportunity is often subordinated to winning the competition and succeeding. Team exercises intertwine student fates so that getting along with teammates and helping them accomplish is the only way to get a good group grade, which is essential for graduating with a good job. Teamwork is a means to an end, and too often a time-consuming one that students dread.

People Skills Acquired for Getting Along with Cohorts

Managers with a record for getting things done without their manager having to spend much time reviewing their work, or having to perform an extensive amount of damage control, are given additional responsibilities and promoted. Managers who require oversight and aren't able to keep the background noise down eventually fall by the wayside.

Progressing up the ladder, managers find themselves balancing multiple commitments, any one of which could monopolize their time. They are constantly encountering situations unlike anything they've previously experienced. Required are people skills far more nuanced and sophisticated than the line-authority dictums that gave them sway with direct reports. Most provocatively, they find themselves challenged by cohort managers making demands they lack the means to redirect or control.

Further complicating matters is the growing realization that the opinions these cohorts form of them substantially determine how they are viewed and valued company-wide. With direct reports, managers can assert themselves and insist that things be done the way they believe is right. But with cohorts, they risk damaging their good image each time they express a differing viewpoint, or fail to give someone the response that person wants. They find themselves in long meetings groping to decide which variation of some way of concluding, that doesn't seem viable to them, will be deemed "best" by the group—just because no one strenuously dissented. The pressure to avoid conflict and homogenize their views eventually becomes so great that they start losing track of what they truly believe is correct.

Gradually, managers get the message about what their next promotion depends on. They learn that building genial relationships and managing their image is every bit as important as accomplishing company-desirable results. They begin seeing a political dimension to everything they say and do. Suddenly work life is less spontaneous and everything is calculated.

Few managers appreciate the irony of the "loss of power" feeling that moving up the management chain causes in them. How can they assert themselves when the people they're working with, whose opinions about them matter so much, appear overly sensitive, judgmental, and competitive? As if all this wasn't constraining enough, they find their candid off-the-cuff comments of frustration getting them into trouble. As a result, they lose their spontaneity and affect a subdued persona—which is another irony. Being subdued is viewed as a positive quality. Peers and higher-ups don't see them "holding back." They see them "maturing." Now they're team players and—get this one—"low maintenance" for upper-level managers. Most ironic of all, and most managers would see this if they were to stop and think about it, is that nothing they accomplish seems to matter unless the person viewing it likes them personally.

Thrown into such politicized waters, managers have little choice but to swim. On their minds is playing it cool long enough to get promoted to the top tier, where they can be the ones whose sensitivities are respected, and whose judgments count. Their energies are focused on making people feel good when they're around. Finding out what people need in order to feel good in their presence requires a new level of sensitivity, especially to what they see implied by a person's affect and behavior, and not explicitly verbalized. Without realizing what they're doing, they find themselves enrolled in work-culture "charm school."

Their needs immediate, the messages get through. "Soften your tone, polish rough spots; don't be so direct, leave people an out; be seen associating with people of stature and power; keep your hands away from your face when you talk; hide anxiety; sound confident; dress up when making a presentation and limit your slides to a half dozen; expand your network; never pass on an opportunity to compliment someone; make sure people get your name; don't over-cc your emails, but make sure everyone who sees themselves relevant gets one; dumb it down but not too much; don't repeat to emphasize; if you think you can get your point across by hinting, give it a try, but then make sure they got it right." This is the new people-skill education managers get. Think what you want about it, but I don't find it much different than what MBA students learn about getting along with cohorts, and managing their image, in their socialization at school.

Life at the Top Isn't All It's Cracked Up to Be

Moving up the ranks, finally making it to the top tier, it's natural for managers to think they've been around long enough to make an easy transition to their new assignment. They see a lot going for them. They have many long-term relationships, and firsthand knowledge of how managers below them think. They know how the system works, and there are plenty of people whose capabilities they know well. For years they've had pockets of organizational ineffectiveness in their sights, but lacked the authority to fix what they saw as broken. Emboldened by their top-tier clout, they feel confident asserting their ideas and redirecting people accordingly. Best of all, they can relax and enjoy hanging out and bantering with company friends. The sigh of relief is almost audible in this excerpt from an email sent to me by a newly appointed top level manager.

> I was particularly struck by a comment you made in the SLC [Senior Leadership Committee] meeting when you critiqued middle management requiring more "image" than "authenticity," and "relationships of substance."

I kept thinking how my ability to say the right thing, to withhold negative feelings and emotions, and to connect with others in shallow but pleasant ways has fostered my success in the company. No wonder my years have taken such a toll—I'm drained from carefully and constantly managing how people see me.

After the meeting I ran into a woman with whom I spent a year working when on assignment in Seattle, who now is working here. Because of what you said I decided to share something I normally withhold. I told her how exhausted I was and that I had somehow managed to hold on long enough to get this promotion. She expressed surprise, saying she always saw me as someone who had it together and made everything look easy. I told her it's an image I worked hard to project, and that my avoidance of sharing struggles, and what challenges me, is a defense. After a few more minutes of conversation, she thanked me for sharing, and invited my wife and me over for dinner with her and her husband. It was an honest invitation, not the superficial "Oh we should hang out." I felt she was reaching out to provide an opportunity for more realism. I look forward to keeping authenticity in focus and am questioning how I can utilize more of it in my new sphere of influence.

Although it is perhaps a bit more dramatic than some, I found this email fairly describing what many managers think is possible when first assuming jobs at the top.

Asserting themselves and beginning to make improvements, newly promoted top-tier managers find their experiences deviating considerably from what they expected. The changes they initiate, that seem so logical to them, appear to unnerve the people they were counting on to carry them out. People lower down seem resistant to leaving their comfort zones—fearful of exposing limitations that in the current schema they are able to keep hidden. They get pushback from people they never suspected were so defensive. Engaging people they believed to be in-company friends, whom they knew well and worked with for years, they find themselves back at square one, attempting to re-establish trust. Too much of what they thought they knew, that led to their feeling secure in their elevated job, turns out to be incorrect. All of a sudden they're unsure. Here's a vignette that graphically illustrates what I'm describing. It was told to me by an ad agency executive a short time after he was elevated to chief operating officer.

> For years I looked at our account managers quite critically. Their clients never seemed to know how our agency worked, or how we priced their projects. And they always seemed so vague when presenting their clients' needs inside the agency. During meetings they were always telling clients not to worry—that what was planned for their campaigns wouldn't go over budget. But it always did.
>
> After being promoted I found individual meetings with these guys a very pleasant surprise. My respect grew considerably and I began thinking that I had them all wrong. Then something happened in a client meeting. I forget exactly what was said, but it caused me to question my change of heart. I realized the reason I looked forward to meetings with these guys individually was that they only brought good news, and always said flattering things about me. I saw that I was right about how I initially saw them. These guys don't know our business. They make a living off of their ability to tell clients what they want to hear. And our clients are nuts about them. So who am I to complain?

Teamwork at the Top

Wouldn't you think by the time a manager reaches the top tier that their number one priority would be total-entity results and overall company well-being? Many people think it should be that way, and probably no one wants this more than the CEO, who's on the hook for everything that happens in the company. That person counts on top-tier reports placing company interests ahead of any jurisdictional accomplishment.

No CEO wants the marketing department to meet its goals by pushing last year's models at the expense of new-direction products, just because they're easier to sell. No CEO wants to see top-tier managers engaged in turf wars, and struggling with one another for dominance. They need managers at the top viewing every decision, and action contemplated, from an enterprise-first-and-foremost perspective.

Intellectually, every top-level manager agrees. No one says anything different. Of course company interests supersede any jurisdictional predilection. But this is not what most top-level managers practice. The perilous journey they took to get to the top has left them determined to never leave themselves vulnerable again. No matter how dire the entity situation, or great the opportunity, they cling to survival mantras: "never miss your numbers"; "accomplish everything you, and the units reporting to you, have been assigned and agreed to"; "allow no one to encroach on, or exercise, your authority"; and "don't confront any jurisdictional leader with facts they don't want others to see them knowing." Yes, sacrifice for the greater good, but only after jurisdictional interests are secured. When the company doesn't do well, managers expect to feel some pain. But when their jurisdiction doesn't meet expectations, they fear more than pain. They fear career morbidity.

Even if CEOs realized all I've alleged, and many do, their need for entity-first support is so great that most can't help but get seduced by their own desires. They don't realize it's their doubts, not their positive convictions, that have them anointing top-level managers as the company's senior leadership team. Initially flattered by the stature bestowed on them, top-tier managers soon find themselves committed to what many complain is an endless stream of unnecessary meetings. But the CEO sees these meetings as essential to top managers internalizing an entity-first orientation. Minimally, the meetings are an opportunity to get them all in the room to jointly scrutinize for instances of someone's not walking the company-first talk.

Discussed are all matters impacting company operations and profitability, tactical and strategic, present and future. I've observed and consulted to CEO-led teams in dozens of companies and, specific hot issues notwithstanding, I find few differences in CEO motives. All want, and urge, their top-level managers to speak up on matters extending beyond their jurisdiction. No CEO likes to see any individual mincing words or playing it safe. Many count on outlier viewpoints, and the interplay of top-level managers' opinions, for sounding-board advice and a pulse-taking perspective of what people deeper down in the organization are thinking. And CEOs like to assume that the logic behind any jointly decided matter will trickle out into every work unit and activity.

Unfortunately for CEOs and their companies' shareholders, most top-level managers are so snakebitten and security oriented that they are unwilling to put jurisdictional matters on hold, no matter how compelling the company priority. As well-intentioned as any might be, I've seen many top managers who think they've fully joined up overlook visible signs of their own resistance. Saying all the right words, they resist giving others deep windows into jurisdictional affairs, won't take controversial stands, and don't ask other-revealing questions. Lots of luck to any CEO naïve enough to expect candid discussions in senior leadership team meetings.

So who gets taken in most—the CEO or that person's senior-level managers? In most instances it's the CEO, especially if it's a person brought in from outside the company. It's not that the CEO can't succeed without receiving more candor. It's that the CEO should not be working under the illusion that top managers, who seem happy to do their bidding, feel sufficiently secure to trust that CEO with their back—especially when that person is a newcomer.

Case Study

For an in-your-face example of what I'm describing, consider a situation that took place at the Tribune Media Company–owned *Los Angeles Times*. It's one I learned about when a reporter called requesting my reaction to the newly announced change in the company's vacation policy and the outrage it incited in employees. Here's how the debacle played out.

> Late afternoon November 13, 2014, every *LA Times* supervisor, manager, and salaried employee received an email "introducing a new Discretionary Time Off (DTO) policy." Sent from "Internal Communications,"[3] it described, in two-thousand-word detail, a new vacation policy that would take effect six weeks later, on January 1. Instead of accruing a set number of vacation days each year, to use or bank, employees desiring time off would merely ask their boss. If they could be spared, the request would be granted. Employees could have time off whenever they needed it, and the company would realize a substantial savings by taking a huge and growing banked vacation charge off its ledger. Simple and straightforward, a win for everyone. Right?
>
> The reason I was asked to comment was that employees were going berserk. Supervisors and managers were affected and no doubt they were upset as well. They too would have to petition their boss for time off. Thinking the plan bizarre, they couldn't complain out loud. Every career-oriented manager knows complaining is not a smart thing to do.
>
> Having survived extreme cutbacks in staffing during the 2008 recession, most employees were experienced professionals. From my knowledge of news

organizations, these had to be smart, savvy people fully capable of envisioning more negatives than just being "gypped" [in the words of one staffer who spoke to me] out of time off. No doubt many feared the added muscle their direct overseers were getting that could be used to intimidate them on any matter, and the ingratiating, boot-licking behavior in store for them when petitioning for time off. Then think of what's ahead for the overseers—managers and supervisors—and the pressure they'd be under not to go too deep into the time-off allotment budget that had to exist, even though it hadn't been mentioned. Imagine the storytelling they'd have to go through justifying why they weren't overstaffed yet could do without the people to whom they granted leave, all the while defending themselves against accusations of leniency and favoritism shown. No matter which end of the lens you looked through, this DTO was an absurdity from inception.

Sometimes sanity restores quickly; happily this is such an instance. But a lot of damage was done during the eight days that passed prior to a bolt-of-lightning edict telling everyone the plan was rescinded.

Let's examine how this situation unfolded and why top-level managers, who must have known employees wouldn't like the DTO plan, allowed it to go forward. No doubt a plan such as this starts at the very top, and at the *LA Times*, that's the person holding the title of publisher and CEO. On the job just three months, this individual was not only new to the paper but new to the publishing industry. A quick examination of his credentials depicts him as a banker who made millions on Wall Street and then acquired a good deal of civic knowledge working as the dollar-a-year deputy mayor of Los Angeles. A philanthropic giver, he sat on the boards of several art and social service nonprofits. Truly a man for all seasons, he arrived with many high-stature connections.

Then there was the CEO's "right-hand person" for day-to-day administrative and management advice. At least that's what the title "Senior Vice President (SVP) for Administration and Human Resources" communicates to me. Prior to stepping up, she spent over a decade heading the company's HR function, and had been with the company several years before that. I'd say that's more than enough time to know how mid- and lower-level managers, supervisors, and salaried employees might react to a DTO plan. If there was anyone savvy enough to use the pseudonym "Internal Communications" to keep their name off the initial announcement people received, it had to be her. Apparently, the switch to DTO was the new CEO's idea, and she went along.[4]

For me, the smoking gun exposing the SVP's complicity in going along with the CEO's idea and being reluctant to assert herself—even though that's what someone in her role should be doing—came three days after the announcement in a follow-up sweet-talking email sent to all exempt employees, this time under her own signature. Aimed at quelling the ruckus, she wrote a simply stated "taste it, you'll like it" message. But taste was not what employees were objecting to. They didn't like the way it smelled! No doubt most, if not all, other top-level managers were consulted. They had to be. The policy change affected every non-union person working at the *Times*. Any manager inclined to speak up would have had a pretty easy time making a case against this action. But apparently no one did, at least not forcefully enough to make a difference.

Now for the grand finale. Did anyone at the top stand accountable? Which top-tier samurai had the integrity to fall on their sword? No, outside of what I told you up front about having the change rescinded, you get none of the accountability you might expect. Not even an apology for the upset caused.

The rescinding notice did not come from the *LA Times* CEO, and it did not come from the SVP. Embarrassingly, it came from the big boss in Chicago, the publisher and CEO of the

Tribune Media Company, the man who hired the *LA Times* CEO. He wrote a hail-fellow-well-met "Message from Jack" email, addressing the complaining throng as "Colleagues." Not one to beat around the bush, he covered over the matter succinctly. Check out his first paragraph.

> Colleagues:
>
> The change in policy outlined in the note created confusion and concern within the Company. The purpose of this note is to let you know that, based on valuable input from employees, the DTO policy is rescinded.

No ambiguity here. Then, after three equally short and blah paragraphs, he closes out with:

> Thank you for your understanding and continued commitment to helping shape our new Company.
>
> Best,
>
> Jack

Fiasco come and gone, researching this case I find no involvement whatsoever by the *LA Times* publisher and CEO, who, in my mind, had to be the biggest culprit of them all. Looking back, I see his fingerprints on this plan when, three months earlier, in an *LA Times*–published article, he described his mission. Referring to his job as publisher, he said, ". . . it's an organization that has to change in order to prosper. If they're looking for a caretaker they picked the wrong man."[5]

Unfortunately, for *Times* employees, it seems they did get a *care taker*. He took a lot of *care* avoiding responsibility for the debacle he initiated. Minimally, he should have learned an important lesson from the circle-the-wagons action his boss took protecting him. Jack knew he had a dog in the fight and, in the service of helping "colleagues," knew how to keep that dog safe—this time. On the other hand, guess who's coming

to work at the *Times* as a top-tier—may I use Jack's term—
"colleague," with duties not initially specified? An industry-
savvy, recently retired, long-time senior editor from the
world-class-managed *New York Times*. Perhaps he was sent as
a CEO "minder." Or perhaps for "bench strength," just in case
Jack concludes a replacement is needed.

Insecurity at the Top

Being a top-level manager in a profitable company, or in a nonprofit without financial woes, is not enough to prevent managers from feeling insecure when their boss asks them to identify
a backup and make sure that person is sufficiently trained. I've
already covered the main stressor. It only takes one person to
fire them—the CEO. But usually that threat is readily managed: make sure you bring in expected results, be forthright
and honest in stating your problems, and lack a backup sufficiently skilled to replace you.

Good-hearted or bad-hearted, living the top-tier life—pay
increases and bonuses paid for results, expense account–
supported good living, savings accumulating, and lifestyle
going up—many managers fear having people around who
are able to do their job and for less pay. In response, I've seen
many managers gravitate to a self-protective routine for job-
security insurance. It's one I recognized almost as soon as
I saw it because I grew up seeing it applied. In fact, until I saw
it used in companies, I thought my Aunt Bessie invented it.

My mother, Rose, had two sisters, Kate and Bessie. Each
of them was a to-die-for baker. Of the three, Bessie was the
best. Her Chicagoland baking reputation challenged Julia
Child's. Everyone who tasted one of her pies, her bread, or
a cake claimed they had never eaten anything comparable.
Smart people were always asking for her recipes, and Bessie
generously gave them out. But, as only our immediate family knew, there was a reason why no one's baking ever held a
candle to Aunt Bessie's. Turns out the people asking for recipes

weren't so smart, because none of the recipes Bessie gave out were precisely the ones she used. Writing them down, Aunt Bessie always left something out, or adjusted the quantity of an ingredient.

Many top-tier managers act similarly. People groomed as their backups are periodically staged to screw up. It's done differently each time, and almost always in a multi-party setting, where backups are either asked to explain something they're unprepared to do, or report on a project about which they've been provided incorrect or insufficient information. Thus, up until the day a top-tier manager decides to leave, their backups never appear *quite ready* to replace them.

Conclusion

I don't think many well-intentioned people who become managers expect the travails I've laid bare in this chapter. I've cast the motivation for managers acquiring people skills as more for image and defense against criticism than for facilitating employee effectiveness. My portrayal depicts managers as far more vulnerable and insecure than they, or anyone else, wants to see them. Now for the bad news. I've barely scratched the surface. More perils than I've alluded to face managers in their quests to feel sufficiently secure to give employees the good management behavior they deserve. That's what I'm out to explain in the next two chapters, the first of which is based on a supposition that I bet most readers will find a stunning, although plausible, surprise.

Notes

1. Perhaps in another life I'll write a book-length version of the flimflam that goes on when managers are selected. For our purposes here, I'm ready to stand my ground in asserting that interpersonal skills and management training are the fix after a problem surfaces, and not primary considerations in the selection process of a manager.

2. According to a Graduate Management Admission Council study. M. Murray, *Business Education & Administration* 3, no. 1 (2012): 29–40.

3. A function that didn't formerly exist and is not identifiable on any organization chart.

4. Not to mention checking the legality of the DTO policy, getting buy in from all top-tier managers, and drafting it for public consumption.

5. Christopher Goffard, "Austin Beutner Named Publisher and CEO of Los Angeles Times," *Los Angeles Times*, August 11, 2014.

Part II

IS BAD MANAGEMENT HERE TO STAY?

4

WHY MANAGERS FEEL SO VERY VULNERABLE

Let me pose a not-so-hypothetical question. Assume there was a corporate practice that damaged the relationship between bosses and their subordinates, kept employees from speaking honestly about themselves and company practices, helped bad managers be bad managers and hindered good managers from being good managers, and ultimately hurt the bottom line. Further assume that there wasn't a shred of evidence that anything good came out of this practice.

What do you think managers would do?

Nothing, it seems. Exhibit No. 1: the performance review, a practice that is as destructive and fraudulent as it is ubiquitous. And despite all the evidence— despite the fact that almost every person reviewed and every person reviewing knows that it is bogus— corporate bosses do nothing to hasten its demise. They won't even acknowledge that they have a problem.[1]

I'm sobered by a career spent exposing the negatives in mainstream good management practices, mistakenly assuming that well-intentioned managers would revise their erroneous ways once they realized the negative effect they were having. It's not that I've gotten much pushback about the dysfunction I've exposed, or disagreement about what revisions would be in everybody's best interests. Yet despite all the good intentions, little gets altered. Apparently, the practices I've been urging managers to revise are much too insidious and culturally embedded for any manager, or ad hoc group of non-top-level managers, to change on their own.

Don't get me wrong. I'm not a world-of-work Father Flanagan[2] contending there's no such thing as a bad manager—just managers who inadvertently do some bad things. That's not at all what I think. Yes, there are some mean-spirited, insensitive, selfish, and incompetent managers who feel no guilt or shame for the negatives their bad behavior inflicts. I think Lord Acton had it correct when he warned that "power tends to corrupt, and absolute power corrupts absolutely." Organizations have a way of unleashing power-hungry bullies who, misusing their rank, perform payback beatings, perhaps for the ones they suffered as children. It's not my intent to ignore what they do. The problem is that they look like the rest of us, and sometimes we miss recognizing them until their dirty work is done. In fact, I'd like to make a plea to religious people reading this book. See if you can get your chosen deity to turn every mean-spirited manager's left ankle so we see them coming, and can run like hell before they start berating us with their "right."

I empathize with the vast majority of managers who mean well but can't emancipate to act differently. I see them stuck between the proverbial rock and hard place. Their companies reward managers for racking up accomplishments far better than they reward creating the circumstances for others to accomplish and succeed. It's analogous to professional football. Players who cross the goal line carrying the ball get big paychecks, while the players whose blocking makes it possible for them to score get pats on the back. Dreams to realize, mortgages to pay, and families to support, managers aren't in a position to look out for employees if it means forgoing the rewards they seek. Quickly managers learn to look out for themselves first, because who else will? In today's competing-for-credit work environment it's seldom the higher-level person to whom one reports.

It's no wonder so many managers feel vulnerable when the topics of management styles and management practices are raised. Deep down, most managers know what they're doing is more "right" for themselves than for their employees. And deeper down, they know that whatever they're attempting to do is more about *being seen* as doing things right than actually doing what's right for the company. Most managers feel too vulnerable to think things through for themselves. Under so much pressure to appear how they're supposed to be—you know, like objective—it's easy for managers to lose track of what they authentically think and feel.

Self-interested pursuits are natural; they're everyone's top priority. But self-interests are prohibited in the workplace out of fear that people might put what's self-advantageous ahead of what the company needs. This applies to fiscal gain, and it also applies to a manager putting self-advancement and accomplishing ahead of looking out for employees.

Sadly, it doesn't stop with the workplace prohibiting self-interested pursuits. The work culture also has people convinced that being genuine and heartfelt—yes, authentic—is risky. It bullies people into hiding their beliefs, insecurities, and ambitions, because everything has to be *objective*. To be personally involved is unprofessional. And even though self-interests are often cited as a top-priority motivator, they're not to be explicitly acknowledged. Thus, managers don't feel they can show their real colors. Instead, they puff up their chests and, concealing their flaws and exaggerating their strengths, they wear masks and put on performances. As you can imagine, this leaves managers with a lot of guesswork, trying to contemplate what their peers know about them. I don't know about you, but I much prefer playing charades at home with friends than with people at work—especially while trying to get important things accomplished.

So let's peel the onion back an additional layer to understand just what it is about the pretense of objectivity that has so many well-meaning managers on edge.

Cultural Expectations Make Managers Fear One Another

When I reflect on the abundance of mismanagement behavior I observe, the verbal tiptoeing and doublethink explanations managers use to justify the negatives in their behavior, and their reluctance to correct practices that are blatantly wrong, my analysis always leads to the same conclusion. The underlying cause for managers continuing with practices that systemically block employees from being their most effective, from speaking their minds, and from working independently, is *insecurity*. And while there are as many sources of insecurity as there are managers—insecurities due to job demands, faulty performances, and the remnants of life situations faced past and present—I find insecurity resulting from a manager's fear of a competence-disparaging attack from a cohort manager to far exceed insecurity arising from any other source.

That's right. Strange as it may sound, I find most managers unnerved by the ever-present possibility that something they say or do, however inadvertently, will prove so unnerving to a cohort that it will set that cohort off on an aggressive course of criticism—using accusations and innuendo to malign the manager's image, and to devalue the work they perform.

What's ironic is that the criticisms I find managers fearing most from a cohort are provided by what the work culture falsely idealizes—criticisms for not being objective, being emotionally involved, acting with bias, and for the clandestine pursuit of self-interested agendas. Managers are also vulnerable to accusations that they've self-conveniently crafted their work style to align with skills they possess, with minimal need for skills they see themselves unable to master. Ridiculous as it may seem, managers fear cohorts assailing them for being flawed, imperfect, emotional, nonobjective, and self-interested.

Wait, did you catch that? Managers are afraid of being seen acting human!

The provocation for an attack might be anything a cohort finds threatening. Perhaps it's for objecting to a plan in which a cohort was self-interestedly invested; perhaps for saying something a cohort took as image-diminishing, or disparaging their value to the company; perhaps for demonstrating a skill or competency that a cohort sees as competitive with their expertise; perhaps for taking an action a cohort saw encroaching on his or her domain of authority. Whatever the provocation, the cohort's reaction won't necessarily be a valid reading of a manager's actions or intent. Moreover, and here's one you can take to the bank, the cohort's criticism is all but guaranteed to be based on grounds unrelated to what set them off. Whatever misbehavior is cited, the cohort will allege their criticism "objective," and totally aligned with company-needed outcomes.

Talk about insecurity stemming from capable cohorts demeaning one another! Take a look at this story related by a young professional who is struggling, wanting to keep her firm on track, because managers above her were locked in a competition she saw jeopardizing everyone's hard work and chances for success. Why do these managers treat one another as she describes? What blocks them from agreeing to disagree, and working together for the company's sake? Here's how this professional wrote her concern to me:

> I work in management consulting, which is all about sales. Everything we do, every conversation we have is aimed at getting the next engagement. My firm may soon acquire the biggest sale in the history of the company—which seems like a good thing but may ultimately tear us apart.
>
> Two managers above me own client relationships that are critical to our group's existence. One has a pending sale from a Fortune 500 company that will be the biggest we've ever received. If this happens, both managers

will be made partners, but these women constantly clash. They undermine one another with their staffs and always look for an opportunity to get ahead of the other. I'm totally perplexed by the slandering criticisms they levy, and can't figure out why they refuse to cooperate. We're on the same team, right? Working in factions is not going to get us that sale, and both of them, along with the rest of us, will suffer.

I have casually mentioned how our team should work together to "expand the pie" and not compete against each other for one tiny slice. This is only in everyone's best interests. But my comments make no difference. What else can I do in my current role to make our team operate effectively? This is an interesting and vexing experience for me because I cannot fathom why my team, particularly these two individuals, let personality clashes and a competitive streak get in the way of something that obviously benefits everyone.

Clearly, there's no trust between these feuding managers, or probably, for that matter, among many others in the firm. Instead of trying to understand one another's needs, and probe the reasons for their differences, these managers spend their time looking for opportunities to devalue one another's work and reputation. But for what purpose, and at what cost? Just imagine what a different and healthier workplace everyone would have if these managers spent as much time and effort improving protocols and practices as they do cutting one another down.

This brings me to a poignant question—why would a preponderance of managers feel vulnerable to trumped-up charges to the point where they are profoundly and perpetually insecure? Aren't manifest competencies and established value to the company enough to keep one safe from reproach? Can people making important contributions actually find themselves devalued on a whim?

Managers would like to believe that demonstrated value in producing important results can withstand self-serving, trumped-up criticism. But I find most managers see themselves vulnerable to capricious labeling. They may say they believe something different, but that's not how most behave. They walk on eggshells. Maintaining a vigil, they respect other people's sensitivities, conduct themselves "professionally," and go all out in observing political correctness. Good luck getting to know anyone's true self in this kind of work environment.

Nothing Is Objective . . . Nothing!

Feeling vulnerable, managers avoid owning up to and expressing what they truly think. They speak in the third person, use the king's "we," and communicate in a style that makes mere opinions sound like established fact. Now let me tell you an actual fact, since we're speaking factually. Nothing in people's behavior at work—absolutely nothing—is objective. The same events, the same words, the same anything will be seen and interpreted differently according to the mind-sets, motives, and background of each participant and observer.

There's little to debate. Subjectivity, personal bias, and self-interests are inevitable and, yes, natural. Subjectivity colors each person's perception and assessment of every work situation, with interpretations as different as the lives people lead. Apparent or not, every preference that's shown, every decision that's made, and every judgment that's rendered is shaded by inner attitudes, whether or not an individual is aware of their influence and actually believes their opinion grounded in objective fact. Often, the extent of the shading is determined by who else is present and the amount of self-serving distortion the individual believes he or she can get away with, given what the people in the room know and believe. It's what the market will bear.

Claiming to be "objective" implies that all "unbiased" people will see events as the objective-alleging person views them, will characterize what they see in similar terms, will attribute the same meaning and significance to what they believe is transpiring, and that any differences in perceptions and interpretation can be discussed rationally and reconciled. But this is never the case. I mean, it takes decades for historians to get history they personally witnessed into some semblance of even-handed perspective and agreement.

Just implying objectivity, let alone asserting that a depiction of human events is objective fact, flies in the face of experimental social science. What actually transpires is exemplified in such popular psychological canons as "motivation determines perception," "where you stand determines what you see," and "you can forget the past but the past doesn't forget you." Just because someone fails to recognize the personal needs prompting their actions, or the past experiences coloring their sentiments, does not negate subjective forces as drivers. People go into therapy, engage in consciousness-raising, and watch political debates to see beyond their personal filters. There's a saying that people who decry psychotherapy like to use: "analysis is paralysis." Nuh-uh. That doesn't fly with the psychologist in me. I think that failing to recognize the subjective forces directing a person's actions is a sentence for that person to repeat mistakes of the past. This reminds me of a cousin who married and buried three guys named Stan, despite the fact that when introduced to the third, I urged that Stan to run.

If you need more, think of it this way. Everyone's perspective is as unique and different as their thumbprints. Take any topic or social issue where people's opinions differ: politics, sporting events, gay marriage, healthcare, gun safety, vaccinations, et cetera. Even movies are a good example. Every day people go to the same movie and walk out with completely different opinions. They saw the same actors, listened to the same lines, and ate popcorn from the same concession stand. But one person could hate the film and demand a refund while another could say it was as profound and as meaningful as any film they'd ever seen. Whatever their opinion, no matter how strongly believed and vigorously expressed, it is not objective.

Seldom stated as starkly as how I think it needs to be emphasized here, the mainstream work culture requires managers to buy the belief that *outlawing subjectivity makes subjectivity disappear*. But banning subjectivity doesn't make it disappear any more than the prohibition was able to ban alcohol and make it disappear. Outlawing subjectivity only drives it underground, which is where managers keep it. Its constant presence is easily viewed in the words that top-level managers speak, and in what you see them actually doing when they tell you they're doing something else. It's even easier to detect in what's spoken by managers lower down.

The performance review is the worst example of what is often held up as "objective" because one imperfect manager's biased opinion of an employee's imperfections gets represented in the employee's file as a truthful, objective fact—not a self-serving opinion. To be fair, any evaluation should include the personal preferences and comfort zones of the manager assigning the ratings, and the fact that the rating system allows one manager's high-scoring "team player" to qualify as another manager's low-scoring "conflict-avoider." Here's another fact. Employees receiving reviews from multiple managers will, more likely than not, receive significantly different scores from each. In science that's called "lack of inter-rater reliability." And in science, that lack serves to invalidate all subsequent conclusions drawn.

I often hear managers using terms like *objective* and *fact-based analysis,* and hear of performances quantified in percentages and statistics, as if these terms and numbers eliminate the subjective element. It's a well-known fact that even scientists place the most emphasis on the numbers that support what they think, and downplay the ones that question or contradict their beliefs.[3] The point is that any characterization made by one manager of another is subjective and wouldn't hold up as scientifically valid in any court of law. Their representations are based on their own points of view and life experiences. Managers open themselves to criticism each time they present self-convenient beliefs and opinions as hard fact. All it takes to invalidate their conclusions is for someone to point out the self-serving motives behind their beliefs, and then depict what they have to gain.

What gets termed "reality" at work results from tacit politicking, as stakeholders vie and negotiate to get events and actions labeled to reflect their individual—and hidden—agendas. Of course, what's agreed to, both in terminology and valuing of an activity, will usually be less than what any stakeholder actually believes. In the workplace, few facts speak for themselves. Facts are used, ignored, and labeled to support how people with complementary personal agendas have tacitly agreed to speak about what's taking place—despite disparities in personal views.

How Objectivity Leads to Vulnerability

Taking care not to veer far from work-culture-stipulated good management behavior, managers are ever pretending their viewpoints and actions are objective, and free of self-interested gain. They frame their advocacies impersonally, as if what they are saying is "the only right decision to make," "the absolute best action given our goals and resources," "what the marketplace requires," and "the only tried-and-true way to get results." Using such phrasing allows managers to gain plausibility for just about any action they want to take. Likewise when accounting for mistakes made, and undesirable results. All that's necessary to avoid criticism and blame is being able to credibly allege one acted objectively, doing what was best for the company—coupled with sufficient organizational power to deter cohorts with competing interests from objecting.

If you think having to live with managers playing mind games is bad for employees, it's worse for the managers who have to live with and defend them. To maintain credibility, managers have to constantly pretend that everything they stipulate is based on objective fact—which, of course, it never is. Since all people—even managers—are subjectively-driven beings, they're never going to be objective no matter how convincingly they pretend.

Constant pretending puts managers in tough spots. They find themselves out on a limb knowing that anyone seeing subjectivity, or self-interest gain, in what they advocate as good for the company has grounds for thinking them duplicitous, dishonest, or worse. People feeling manipulated, misled, aced out, or taken advantage of get angry—especially when what's being attempted is performed by a person professing objectivity. Depending on the stakes, seeing oneself duped readily sparks an impulse to expose the perpetrator's ruse.

The myth of objectivity leads to expectations no manager can meet—that is, without free-rein use of doublethink. It's as if the work culture at large fears that condoning the everyday presence of self-interested pursuits is tantamount to opening the floodgates of self-indulgent rip-offs. Talk about bankrupt premises. What's to lose by making it possible to discuss and exchange opinions about what each self-interested and biased person sees going on?

While few managers seriously believe that anyone is objective, all managers are under pressure to pretend they are. Some acknowledge their sentiments, inclinations, and personal values in the general case. Everyone reveals something about their biases and needs and, very important, the origins of them, each time they tell a personal background story. But seldom will you hear a manager explicitly acknowledge a specific self-serving element in an action planned or taken. Now, some managers do profess objectivity more earnestly than others, and I find the most earnest are managers who don't know beans about human nature. For them, pretending to be objective accomplishes an additional self-serving motive. It allows them to delude themselves into thinking their inattentiveness to employee needs is acceptable. To me, that's doublethink squared!

This is not to say that managers never have the best interests of the company at heart, nor speak the truth as they know it. The vast majority of managers I know are very fair, take pains in recounting facts as they know them, and are concerned about their employees' interests even while pursuing their own. But communicating the truth as one knows it is seldom the motive driving a manager's portrayal of any event or action taken. More prominent in most depictions is getting another person's buy-in, usually by emphasizing what they guess that individual will find self-beneficial. Ever-present in the back of one's thinking is spinning words and actions for the purposes of getting other parties to agree that the self-interested path they don't admit to taking leads to company-desirable results.

How Adversaries Are Made

Seldom is the mere recognition of self-interests in a manager's advocacies or actions enough to set a cohort off on a campaign to castigate that manager. But trouble is likely once one or more cohorts, either by intuition or tangible evidence, suspect that the self-interests being perused will lead to actions oppositional to what's important to them. With no means for engaging and reconciling hidden differences, the motive to discredit is born.

Lacking specifics, cohorts fear that even a perfunctory inquiry to quell suspicions will alert a manager of imminent danger, possibly prompting a preemptive strike. Cohorts realize the person attacking first has the advantage. Ironically, all indictments are for violations of which every manager is culpable: feigned objectivity, personal blind spots, self-serving pursuits, and lack of some role-essential skill or job-required competency.

Especially in large companies, and in any organization where people see themselves vying for dominance, jurisdiction, assignment, resources, et cetera, managers worry that something they do, however inadvertently, will set off a chain of contentious actions like the disparaging ones I've been describing. And because indicting allegations seldom reflect the concern provoking a cohort to attack, there's little opportunity to learn what the cohort found so threatening, discuss it, and possibly correct a mistaken interpretation.

With so many possible adversaries, a manager can never relax. Drop the pretense, be authentic, state your underlying motives, tell people your true views, and the only thing you accomplish is increasing your chances of being assailed. Can you imagine a situation where a manager expressing his beliefs with conviction encounters a cohort who discredits his views on the grounds that he is "overbearing and argumentative"? Can you imagine a manager seeking to bring out each person's best, listening attentively to other peoples' ideas and asking follow-up questions, finding herself bum-rapped as "a person lacking original ideas"? I can. In fact, I witnessed each quite recently.

The Need to Self-Protect

Most managers realize that reward, promotion, and all forms of personal success are always at stake during office hours. One mistake—just one convincing accusation—can cripple a career and dash one's dreams of success. Giving the work culture the good management behavior it expects requires so much pretense that even the most seemingly confident manager becomes susceptible to bad management accusations and finger-pointing. There's little choice for most managers. Keep your guard up, stay alert, and watch your back.

The last time I asked for a show of hands about this, the majority of full-time professionals and managers taking my leadership class rated "avoiding standing accountable for a mistake" a weightier force than "receiving recognition for a good job performed." If this informal poll is the least bit valid, it shows how insecure people are. How can a person take risks if they fear standing accountable for a mistake?

Taking pains not to provoke, most managers mute their outward affect. They stick with what their peers will find conventional, adhere to norms, meet cohort expectations, and maintain precedent. They speak politely, observe company etiquette, emphasize similarities, and only reluctantly express even watered-down disagreement. They do their utmost to conceal anger, not criticize, and avoid face-to-face venting of frustrations. They spin words and phrases around known cohort sensitivities, and, when initiating work-related discussions, craft their words to maximize agreement. They avoid blaming and holding cohorts accountable.

Wanting to elude conflict, experienced managers voice their criticisms far from earshot of the people they fault. When frustrations build and the need to vent becomes overwhelming, they do so only with selectively chosen third parties. They must be careful. Experience has taught them that criticisms told third parties in confidence often get back to the people assailed.

Conclusion

Eventually, a daunting realization sweeps into most managers' thinking. If they have all they need to cast aspersions on cohorts, then cohorts possess like means for indicting them. All it takes to have one's character and competence maligned is a threatened cohort motivated to expose them for what they actually are.

Ever on the alert, top-tier managers embrace all the safeguards and self-protective routines at their disposal. I'm going to show you precisely how they go about it next.

Notes

1. S.A. Culbert, "Why Corporate Leaders Won't Abolish Performance Reviews," *HBR Blog Network*, September 21, 2010. http://blogs.hbr.org/cs/2010/09/why_corporate_leaders_wont_ abo.html#comments

2. Edward J. Flanagan was an Irish-born priest who founded a center for troubled youth known as Boys Town in Douglas County, Nebraska. Seeking donations, he coined the slogan, "There is no such thing as a bad boy." https://abbey-roads.blogspot.com/ 2009/05/there-is-no-such-thing-as-bad-boy-fr.html

3. I. Mitroff and R.O. Mason performed what for me was a revealing study on the lack of objectivity amongst scientists. "On Evaluating the Scientific Contribution of the Apollo Moon Missions via Information Theory: A Study of the Scientist-Scientist Relationship," *Management Science* 20, no. 12 (August 1974): 1,501–13.

5

HOW MANAGERS
SELF-PROTECT

Here's something essential all top-level managers resort to but are reluctant to publically admit. It's a topic I seldom see discussed in management textbooks or brought up in the MBA classroom.[1] A manager's daily viability requires considerable pretense, duplicity, and stealth. That's right: everyday credibility and survival, not to mention performing one's job competently, entails more under-the-radar activity than most managers would like to think. I'm not talking underhandedness, backstabbing, or some deliberate mischief-causing action. I'm talking about the covert actions required for circumventing resistance and getting just about anything important accomplished.

While pretense, duplicity, and stealth are a natural, seamless part of every top-level manager's daily routine, few realize how much of their time, energy, and focus goes into keeping others in the dark. For starters, think about how much time managers spend constructing half-truths and giving off the impression they're divulging everything relevant they know, when they're not; convincing a person they don't like that they are their friend; attending waste-of-time meetings; nodding their head to fake agreement; obfuscating to avoid giving an opinion; preparing just-in-case excuses; apologizing for not responding to an email they unintentionally deleted; enlisting someone to tell a third party something they didn't want to say themselves; covering up for a ducked phone call; pretending to be impressed by a picture of an ugly dog on someone's desk; persuading a person who, first chance they get, they'll throw under the bus, that they're loyal; telling a story that exaggerates their contribution to a positive outcome; asking "innocent" questions to uncover a motive; intentionally leaking a confidential communication; pretending to know what was in a report they didn't read; giving someone a heads up about something that hasn't been announced; sidestepping an argument on an issue they don't think can be reconciled; conducting a conversation in a manner that allows them to deny it ever took place; and generally saying and doing whatever seems necessary to get someone's support for an agenda laced with self-interests that they don't want revealed.

During the Cold War 1950s and '60s, people made jokes about all the plotting, conniving, and conspiring taking place behind closed doors at the Kremlin. I find similar dynamics in executive suites today. However, the only person I hear joking about the deceptive ways managers are forced to operate, and the conspiratorial alliances they've formed, is a fictional guy named Dilbert—whose creator, Scott Adams, makes a good living by his doing so.

"The Work Culture Made Me Do It"

Considering the amount of pretense required for credibility in the mainstream work culture, stealth and deception is the only practical course. With self-interests intertwined in every action taken, and company-first-and-only dedication required, how, without subterfuge, can a manager make everything they do appear objective and "good management behavior" correct? Forced to keep their real motives hidden, managers realize they set themselves up for big problems by divulging anything self-beneficial in their actions.

Wait, there's more. The work culture requires managers to cooperate and appear self-sacrificing while working with cohorts pursuing agendas that compete with their own. Possessing self-limitations and faults of which they are aware, and recognizing that they probably have some they've yet to recognize, managers fear the consequences of cohorts catching a glimpse of even a single deficiency.

Okay, time for a spot quiz. What do you call a manager who believes that cohorts discussing their accomplishments, and their value to the company, will be even-handed, fair-minded, and generous in accepting their imperfections and limitations? I'll tell you what I call a manager naïve enough to think this: "headed for unemployment."

If you don't yet see the need for all the deception, add in a manager's need to conceal personality quirks, troublesome home situations, lifestyle eccentricities, and any problem they believe cohorts could use in faulting them. That's right: in addition to condemning self-interested pursuits, ever-present subjectivity, and skill limitations, the mainstream culture cuts little slack for any deviation from cultural expectations and standards.

I could say more but I've made my point. Managers find themselves made vulnerable by work-culture expectations that don't reconcile with their human essence. They feel too insecure to be open and aboveboard being who they are or stating what they actually see, think, and believe. They're unable to speak candidly about their personal limitations, what they seek for themselves, what they're unwilling to do for others, and what they don't know how to accomplish. They think revealing their motives, and the limits of their commitments to their jobs, would be a death wish fulfilled. In the 1970s and '80s, few professionals at IBM thought they could keep their jobs, let alone get promoted, without taking an empty briefcase home at night, pretending they were going to kiss the kids and go right back to work. Today, there's a term for people who don't take work calls at home or answer emails on weekends. It's *slow-trackers.*

Feeling vulnerable for not being as the culture falsely expects them to be, wanting to deter cohorts motivated to call them out for a deficiency, managers search out behavioral routines that safeguard their vulnerability.

Self-Protective Routines for Safeguarding Vulnerability

Years of observing managers self-protect has led to my accumulating a list of routines that managers use to safeguard themselves from cohorts. Of course, each routine is as unique as the individual implementing it, and nuanced for the distinctive situation and circumstance faced. Nevertheless, I find some routines used so frequently that I suspect almost every manager's repertoire includes a variation of each. Consider the following six and ask yourself if you've seen them used and whether, in some of those instances, the person using them was you.

Routine 1: Speak-No-Evil, Hear-No-Evil, Report-No-Evil Groupthink

Among the routines vulnerable-feeling managers use to protect themselves, I find speak-no-evil, hear-no-evil, report-no-evil groupthink[2] the most egregious. I think most managers feel similarly, since it's rare to find a manager willing to own up to using it. While most admit to observing local culture (read: company) norms and mores—benignly characterizing their actions as "one of the things we do here that we don't speak openly about," or "how our group deals with difficult subjects," or "the elephant that's always in the room when we meet"—managers don't admit to the denial, false posturing, deception, and collusion entailed in this routine.

The groupthink I see taking place is much more than a conflict-smoothing-over affectation. It's wide-ranging deception, and basically dishonest, which makes it anything but benign. Using graphic terms, I see it as managers entering into a collusive mutual-protection pact.

Speak-no-evil, hear-no-evil, report-no-evil groupthink involves a group of cohort managers, usually at the same level, tacitly agreeing not to criticize one another or expose any member's work-culture-stipulated misbehavior. In exchange for a manager overlooking what they see as self-serving in a cohort's portrayal of a situation, or flawed in their thinking; not commenting on visible self-pursuits, skill limitations, and faulty executions; and refraining from pointed criticism when giving feedback, cohorts agree to do the same for that manager.

In other words, a group of cohort managers enter into an unspoken compact to surface-level, blanket-accept what one another says and does, and the justifications given. And this acceptance goes "double" when what's alleged concerns an activity within the domain of a manager's jurisdiction and expertise. A manager hearing a cohort mistake a swan for a duck becomes a mandate for that manager to quack.

The speak-no-evil, hear-no-evil, report-no-evil pact requires go-along-to-get-along relationships. One takes cohorts at their word, refrains from pressing them to discuss topics that cause them discomfort, and avoids calling attention to disparities between what cohorts say about themselves, and the work units reporting to them, and how the discerning manager sees it. Managers may offer "friendly advice," but only if they think it can given without the recipient taking it as a criticism.

Remarkable to me is how this type of collusion gets played out straight-faced, without group members exchanging so much as a wink. The pressure to go along can be so strong that slow-to-catch-on managers find their breaking-ranks comments ignored. Not only are cohorts unresponsive to what they allege, they become cool to anything else they speak. And this deaf-ear sanctioning doesn't cease until the ranks-breaker gives a clear indication of joining the compact.

The most damaging part of this routine is when group members avoid discussing actions and activities they see as detrimental to company results. How do I know that one or another member actually sees what they're not commenting on? Because invoking consultant confidentiality I privately point-blank ask people what they actually see and think is going on. Admitting the importance of speaking up, a manager often tells me they fully intend to do so just as soon as circumstances permit. I also hear from CEOs what mangers tell them when they believe a cohort's errant actions contribute to the ineffectiveness of a work unit for which that manager is accountable. Feeling backed up against a wall, managers act to self-protect their record. They see no option other than to tell their "truths"—truths spun for optimal self-serving effect.

I can think of no better example of the damage this type of groupthink perpetrates than the way General Motors executives behaved when considering whether certain models had recall-requiring defects. To avoid being held accountable, executives engaged in what insiders called the "GM Salute." They would cross their arms and point outward to others, which was the coded way of saying, "It's definitely not me; someone else I can't name is responsible." Also used was the "GM Nod," to signal others that verbally agreeing to a plan for taking corrective action also implied that no one would carry it out.[3]

Situations change, and people have limitations in how long they can keep a lid on themselves, which makes it inevitable that collusive agreements eventually come apart. Additional safeguards are needed, and managers, especially top-level ones, are always looking for additional ways to avoid offending cohorts, and warding off those motivated to assail them.

Routine 2: Be Seen as Hardworking and Overloaded

Many call this self-protective routine *image management*—a terminology I find imprecise and overreaching. The self-portrayals I'm about to describe are specifically aimed at managers showboating their hard work and diligence in an effort to deter cohorts who might be inclined to criticize. Seeking to convince cohorts that they'd have a difficult time making a devaluing allegation stick, and that any attempt to do so could prove credibility-eroding to the accuser, managers amass a record of accomplishments and documented diligence. Using this routine, managers portray themselves as ever-attentive, responsive teammates out to get cohorts just what they need and, get this nuance, *much too overloaded* to take on anything more.

Especially useful in securing the hardworking and over-loaded image are activities and outputs to which numbers and percentages can be attached. Why? Because in a work world characterized by false objectivity, numbers and percentages provide tangible evidence that a manager has delivered all that was promised, and oftentimes even more. Get the number of contact hours high enough, cross charges for services down enough, and provide reports chronicling what's been accomplished thick enough, and a manager has unassailable documentation of efforts expended, progress made, and results delivered. Whether a manager could have worked smarter, managed resources more effectively, or produced results of greater value remain open questions. But the *hard* numbers verify that what was contracted for was delivered, whether or not it was what any individual, or jurisdiction, needed most.

Using this "hardworking and overloaded" routine provides managers an ever-ready excuse for not engaging in unfamiliar activities that might expose a limitation. Self-protectively, a manager reasons, "Why risk credibility on an assignment I have no experience performing?" When asked for such involvement, it's safer to merely say something like, "You're right, it's definitely something the company would benefit from our doing. I wish we had the time to give it a try. Unfortunately, my unit is overloaded. I'd be letting all of us down if I assigned my people more work."

Of course, the responsive way for a manager to engage a cohort with needs, and establish goodwill in the process, would be to assume an other-directed focus, asking questions to learn the cohort's reality and the basis of their needs. Begin by inquiring how that person views their work unit's function and the role that person sees your jurisdiction performing companywide. Find out what they believe they've been receiving and how people in their unit value it. Ask where they see their unit's function headed, and what technological and marketplace changes would cause their operations to change. Find out what else they need to be effective. Get a feel for the distinctive way they reason. Experience their unique style and pay attention to how they react to your attempts to influence them. Why is all this important? Because managers alleging they know what's best for a cohort, prior to that individual relating their views, could give the impression of being out to dominate. It's bad politics to leave someone thinking that your idea of teaming up entails your views dominating theirs.

Unfortunately, taking an other-directed, inquiring, power-sharing approach seems too risky for most managers. Hearing what someone wants, but is not receiving, registers as criticism in many people's minds. What if someone requests what a manager lacks the capability to provide? Fearing the possibility that cohorts might later complain about being turned down for something essential, few risk surrendering control.

Instead of inquiring, managers seize the initiative. Asserting jurisdictional authority, they inform cohorts "here's what your unit needs, and this is what my organization will be doing to accomplish it." Each manager draws on their own inimitable form of "I'm the expert, trust me," or "This is how it's always been done, can't you see we're now doing it better than ever." They essentially tell the cohort, "Cool it, I'm in control."

Routine 3: "You Can Count On Me; I'm a Team Player"

Most managers like to portray themselves as having a self-sacrificing, team-oriented mentality. They look for opportunities to make clichéd statements like, "It's never an inconvenience, I'm always glad to help out," "Don't worry about asking, we all work for the same company," and "I'm just one of the many who did my part." They seek to affect this image in face-to-face discussions, group meetings, and, on occasion, even sell it to themselves. However, if you listen closely to their words, most of the time you'll find the rhetoric used in alleging themselves team players impersonal and imprecise. You'll hear managers mouthing the same gratuitous compliments regardless of what the "team" they're speaking about accomplished, even when that team includes people whose efforts they found insufficient.[4]

Convincing cohorts that one is a team player often entails substantial doublethink. For managers to be convincing, it's best they believe it themselves. Despite competing, they posture as the teammate any cohort should find ideal. Attempting to walk the talk, their gait is as pretentious as their rhetoric.

Thinking about the pretense of team play, I'm reminded of an apocryphal story that has Abe Lincoln questioning a carping constituent. Lincoln asks, "If you call a dog's tail a leg, how many legs does a dog have?" The constituent answers, "Five." Making his point, Lincoln responds, "No, four. Calling a tail a leg doesn't make it one." Likewise, labeling a group of vying, pretentious-speaking cohorts the "senior leadership team" doesn't cause members to think and act collaboratively. They just become slicker at hiding their competition. In a self-interested work world where concealed self-agendas inevitably clash, expressions of team play are often politically correct, hollow statements.

Managers can talk team play as much as they like, but in the end, outside of a few exceptional relationships, it's self-protective participation with pretentious words to indicate they're for one another all the way. This is not to say that managers lack a bonding gene or an intrinsic desire for collegial affiliation, or aren't loyal, won't compromise, or don't find gratification expressing themselves authentically. Most people have these inclinations and sincerely want to help others. But such inclinations are only enacted when relating to people they trust, not cohorts whose hidden self-pursuits and sensitivities have them on edge.

Real team play entails owning up to self-interested pursuits, learning the basis of other people's viewpoints, negotiating with all cards on the table, and feeling appreciated for sacrifices made. It requires managers to trust one another sufficiently to say what they truly believe. Work-culture-required pretense stifles activities like these.

Routine 4: Being Seen as Open-Minded and Willing to Be Influenced

When it comes to open-mindedness, there's a fine line managers walk. They know that getting others to value them requires being seen as strong-willed, self-directed, in possession of real expertise, and uncompromising in keeping work units heading in the right direction. They also know that cohorts with different viewpoints and agendas are looking to influence them and want them open to changing their minds. Too much of the former and a manager will be seen as uncaring, only out for themself, and in need of reining in. Too much of the latter and you've got a weak-appearing individual who, in the extreme, espouses the viewpoint of the last person to whom they spoke. What's the right balance to appear worthy of other people's trust and respect?

Unable to anticipate every stakeholder's concealed agendas, managers make a big show of portraying themselves as ever interested in others' opinions and perspectives, and, get this one, empathetic to their needs and concerns. Profess open-mindedness, look pleasant, nod your head to acknowledge you understand, and generally lead others to think you agree. The solution seems quite simple: maintain your course but don't let anyone see you uninterested in their concerns.

Planning to initiate any action that could perturb one or more cohorts, managers go to lengths seeking guidance and buy-in from everyone affected. When only a few individuals and jurisdictions are involved, a manager holds one-on-ones with each. If it's many, it's more efficient to call a meeting.

Trying to keep things low-key, a manager pretends they're merely data-gathering for purposes of scoping alternatives prior to deciding the *proper* course to take. They go to great lengths to feign open-mindedness even when, as is often the case, the manager's mind is made up, commitments are made, and, practically speaking, there's no going back. While the techniques used for convincing people their views and needs are essential considerations vary, the goal is usually the same. Managers seek to avoid any hard feelings that might accompany people's reactions to what they're being forced to accept.

For the "marks"[5] in this flimflam, the schmooze can be enticing. The manager paraphrases their comments to promote the impression that their viewpoint has been understood and valued. They make a show of taking notes to display the seriousness of the consideration given. They may send out surveys, take straw votes, and solicit comments via email. Whatever they do, in the majority of instances, you'll find managers going out of their way to appear far more open to being influenced than they actually are.

By and large, people are reasonable, and no one expects their opinion to have total sway over what a knowledgeable manager decides within the purview of their authority. It's enough for stakeholders to think that their views were seriously considered. To some extent they're correct—objections raised by one petitioner will be cited as a reason for dismissing the viewpoint of another.

Routine 5: Borrowed-Authority Power-Taking

Here's a highly manipulative, self-protective routine that's relatively new on the work scene, although I'm sure its basic approach has been around from the beginning of time. Since initially spotting it, I see it used with increasing frequency. Lacking a common-usage term, I refer to it as *borrowed-authority power-taking*.[6] It entails managers expropriating the voice of a powerful person to advocate an action that's good for them.

In its simplest form, the routine plays out something like this: "I spoke with Bill, probed his beliefs, and this is how he wants it done." Bill could be the CEO with the power to mandate, the tech expert who people think is the final word, or a witch doctor with powers to hex. Whoever Bill is, if the cohort thinks Bill has the authority and is a person one doesn't want to oppose, there's nothing for the cohort to argue. Never said, but clearly implied in the manager's statement, is this: "If you don't like what I concluded from what Bill said, go argue with him." It's all but been federally mandated.

In contrast to the other routines I've described, this one entails a self-interested manager going on the offensive, intimidating cohorts and staring down their resistance. It gets a manager what they desire without having to stand visibly accountable. Instead of arguing the merits of a self-advantageous action, the manager gets to keep their views and motives hidden, challenging the other person to disobey an anointed authority. Through the use an assumed voice, what's alleged doesn't have to be literal, accurate, or appear aligned with the views of the power-taking manager. The manager might even claim to believe the opposite of the viewpoint referenced, saying something to this effect: "Golfing Saturday with Bill, I did my very best to argue . . . ," concluding with, "I see no other alternative but to go along with what he wants." What's more, there's very little vulnerability—at least the first time a cohort uncovers a misappropriation of Bill's viewpoint. The culprit has a very plausible simple excuse: "I'm glad you caught that; obviously I got it wrong."

Routine 6: Convenient Use of Process and Committees to Feign Fair Play

Calling out this routine can sound so irreverent that I feel the need to defend myself prior to describing it. I believe the vast majority of managers are, in their minds, committed to playing by the rules, believe in just treatment for others, and egalitarian in their thinking. I believe it's only the outliers who seek to always have their way and dominate, and think themselves an elitist class.

But in practice, *egalitarian* does not describe how companies and most organizations are run—nor should it. Hierarchical organizations are meant to operate as autocracies. Each person's authority rightly cascades down from the level above. When someone does it wrong, the person above them, who authorizes their activity and delegates their authority, should also take the heat. That's why CEOs often use the Harry Truman–cited adage, "The buck stops here."

No one serious about the profitability and effectiveness of an enterprise should think what transpires at work is the result of fair-play processes. But top-level managers like to play it both ways. When mandating an action they think controversial, they often hide behind fair-play processes, pretending the action they support was made "objectively" by a committee, or in consultation with others appropriate to the decision made, or dictated by precedent, but certainly not by their acting alone using self-indulgent discretionary power. "Why don't you make the decision? Why use so much *process*?" you might ask them. Their answer is, "Fair play and my need to stay objective require a process."

You don't think your CEO deserves such a high salary. Guess what she says? "I agree with you. I don't think I deserve that much money either. The board's compensation committee, concerned about my retention, forced it on me." Fair-play process used; conversation over.

But who created the list of potential board members, and lobbied behind the scenes for "the right ones'" to be elected? And who kept some suggested candidates off the list? You guessed it: the same CEO who's not responsible for her outrageous compensation package, not to mention the generous golden handshake she'll receive in the event of a forced departure. How does the committee structure appear in the annual report? Independent separation of powers.

It's the same throughout the company. I believe most controversial and emotionally charged issues are decided by
the manager directing the jurisdiction authorized to make
the decision. In one way or another, that manager gets to
make every decision that matters to him or her, starting with
whether to make the decision themself or to invoke a tactically chosen, desired-end-result *process*. The manager might
appoint a committee to study the issue and make a recom-
mendation. Then, stacking the deck to favor the decision he or
she wants, the manager decides who serves on the committee
and who does not. Alternatively, the manager may decide that
the outcome they want is easily justified following precedent,
or by invoking a new and different decision-making criterion.
Is this issue best reconciled by "bending" a rule, and cutting
someone a quid pro quo favor? The idea is always to utilize
the means that lead to a conclusion the person on top finds
desirable.

By means of an example, consider how President Barack
Obama dealt with the director of the Centers for Disease
Control and Prevention when, in the fall of 2014, he lost confidence in the director's handling of Ebola cases. Not wanting to
take congressional heat for having an appointee screw up, the
president invented an "Ebola czar," a person with no authority
and no staff who reported directly to him. Invoking process,
the president took personal control of all decisions made about
how and where people exposed to Ebola would be quaran-
tined and treated. Contending that the matter warranted the
dedicated focus of an expert, he had a plausible excuse for
denying the heavy-handedness of his actions.

It's not possible to stipulate all the so-called feigned fair-play
methods managers use. In the world of large organizations,
people with authority can always find a way to gerrymander
process to ensure someone lower down doesn't make a decision that runs counter to their interests.

Conclusion

My purpose in describing self-protective routines extends beyond demystifying subterfuge to make what's going on more visible. I wanted to reify prominent distractions to managers giving reports the good focus they deserve and need. No wonder so many managers arrive home from work asking themselves, "Why am I feeling so beat up and exhausted when all I did today was go from meeting to meeting?" Consciously, few realize the pressures endured, what it took to remain alert, and how much discipline and nuance was required to go another day unscathed.

We've got one more chapter to go in my awareness-raising portrayal of the force field in which managers operate and the self-focused mentality acquired out of necessity. You can call what managers do many things—surviving, coping, remaining viable, and accomplishing—but please don't use the term "good manager behavior" to describe it. *Real* good management behavior requires an other-directed focus. How do we get that with so many culture forces blocking the way? That's what I take up next.

Notes

1. I did in S.A. Culbert, *Beyond Bullsh*t: Straight-Talk at Work* (Palo Alto: Stanford University Press, 2008). So did Jeffrey Pfeffer in *Leadership BS* (New York: Harper, 2015).
2. Groupthink is a means of harmonizing through conformity in which group members forgo the expression of ideas and views they believe put them out of step with what's mainstream or majority.
3. As described in "Anton Valukas's GM Internal Investigation Report," *New York Times*, June 5, 2014. http://www.nytimes.com/interactive/2014/06/05/business/06gm-report-doc.html
4. Now, there are exceptions and I've written about these. People get exhilarated working on time-bounded project teams with

important missions where people are cut disciplinary authority and no hierarchy is observed. S.A. Culbert and J.B. Ullmen, *Don't Kill the Bosses!* (San Francisco: Berrett-Kohler, 2004).

5. Term used by social scientists and "deceivers" when referring to the people cheated in confidence scams.

6. It's reminiscent of Walter Isaacson's description of Henry Kissinger's negotiation style. See W. Isaacson, *Kissinger: A Biography* (New York: Simon and Schuster, 1992).

6

WHAT PREVENTS GOOD MANAGEMENT

We've outed the enemy. Scrutinized its nature. No question about it. The pretense needed for enacting what the culture erroneously calls "good management behavior" causes well-intentioned managers to behave badly. It emanates from the culture's warped view of human nature, the schooling that emphasizes success, and the accomplishments required for moving up. It's in the role models held up for emulation, and the mentality for evaluating managerial work. It's the double-think managers use to circumvent conundrums created by cultural expectations that make no sense. It's the result of having to conceal sentiments, hide self-interested pursuits, feign objectivity, and the dog-eat-dog system produced by managers having to pretend. It's a by-product of the negative skill sets acquired for hiding imperfections, faking team-mindedness, overriding sensibilities, and living with apprehension about what owning up to a mistake can cost one's career. With so many incoherent expectations ingested, it's no wonder managers lose their grip on human nature facts, and fear being their authentic selves.

Few managers realize how much their thinking has been shaped by forces about which they're unaware. It's the American way to think oneself an independent freethinker. The idea that one might be enacting a script written for avatars doesn't enter most managers' minds.

Being constantly on guard and preoccupied with accomplishing and moving ahead renders managers unable to accurately read the feedback their bad behavior provokes. They misinterpret employees' knuckling under to their brute power as agreement; they treat what's said pretentiously as authentic; and they think of their conflict-avoidant behavior with cohorts as "all-for-one team-play." Always on edge working with cohorts, few managers realize the cause of their apprehension. Constantly engaged in deception, they lose track of inner truths. They forget what they needed working their way up the hierarchy that they couldn't get from their managers. Blithely, they assume capable people can take care of themselves. After all, it's what they had to do.

Too many upper-level managers treat managing as a duplicitous game. Publicly, they take steps to insure employees get in line with mandated rules as the means for giving the company what it needs. They do so fully expecting to exploit and bend those rules for self-interested gain. They use the term *game-changer* to characterize the new ways of operating needed to outshine and distance themselves from the pack. It never occurs to them that the range of possibilities for game-changing might include authentic expression, straight-talk relationships, and truly collaborative team-play.

Even when seeing their actions inflicting harm, managers stay the course. Utilizing doublethink, they adopt a mind-set that makes just about any action acceptable—with negatives justified on the grounds of doing "right" for the company. They self-absolve, thinking themselves company patriots. Occasionally questioning the goodness of what they're doing, they rationalize it's necessary for getting others to respect them, and for keeping their job. It's as if managers have the cultural programming internalized to the point where, stranded on a deserted island and starting from scratch, they would re-create the very system that wreaks so much havoc for everyone, especially themselves. It's all they know. How else can one explain why so many intelligent, well-meaning managers have gone so long not insisting on a better way?

Chris Argyris[1] coined the term *skilled incompetence*, which aptly describes much of what I see thwarting the managerial will for change. Managers have become so proficient at getting people to go along with the culture's erroneous thinking that they see little to gain by changing their ways, and too much to lose if they do. It's the everyday game they're accustomed to playing. After all, it was skilled-incompetence pretending that got them to where they are.

Inauthenticity Breeds Negative Politics

Political vying is a pervasive state of affairs in every organization. What could be more natural than managers attempting to get others to go along with a way of seeing things that leads to outcomes beneficial to themselves? That's what everyone does, even if they're not conscious of the efforts they put into convincing others, or resisting what others allege that doesn't match up with their needs.

The vying can be explicit—viewed in actions taken and self-beneficial views expressed, and argued. It can take place indirectly, by means of innuendo and self-convenient phrasing. It can be implicit in what's not said and what remains undone, or implied in a process that can only lead to a single conclusion. Of course, the meaning people derive from an action or verbal description is usually different from what the communicator was attempting to get across. In any organizational setting, especially ones where people feel the need to hide true sentiments, people almost always put their own interpretations on what others say and do.

You'll find the effort managers put into vying—getting situations self-conveniently framed and labeled, and resisting labels antithetical to their interests—varies with the importance an individual places on the outcomes. The intensity of vying increases when seeing oneself engaged in a zero-sum competition—believing that a cohort's viewpoint prevailing equates to the invalidation of one's own. The intensity decreases when a manager sees a cohort's goals overlapping theirs, and looks for ways of framing events that align interests and reduce the competition.

Highly structured and more defined situations limit the number of people who see themselves gaining from involvement in the competition. Less structured, ambiguous situations attract more participants, since there are more possibilities for conceiving outcomes consequential to a variety of self-interested pursuits.

The stakes in organizational politics are similar to the stakes in public politics: money, power, and stature. In the workplace you might substitute the words *pay, authority,* and *career*. It's roughly the same. In public politics onlookers are always on the alert for actions that compromise the public's interests. In workplace politics, what's self-beneficial is almost always under wraps, which makes it difficult to ensure that what vying parties conclude doesn't exact too much from others, or the company as an entity.

Transparency or Opacity?

With politics inevitable, what remains to be decided is the process vying parties use. Will their discussion take place in the sunshine, affording all stakeholders an opportunity to voice their views, and onlookers the ability to safeguard company interests? Or will the vying take place secretively, backroom style, with some stakeholders excluded and onlookers unable to follow proceedings?

You can count on organizational interests being compromised when the vying takes place out of public view. Under such circumstances there's little likelihood of fair play. Stakeholders are excluded; self-interested pursuits go unchecked; and, by definition, all agreements are collusive. Backroom style, only the people in the room know what's being negotiated, and have an opportunity to advocate for what they want. Those excluded, along with the company, are fortunate to have their interests receive as much as lip-service consideration. And when the word gets out, and it almost always does, neglected stakeholders are resentful and look for opportunities to get even. If good management, other-considerate behavior is desired, you'll find the chances of getting it with backroom politics somewhere between slim and none.

Unlike what takes place in public politics, the discourse in organizations is generally polite. Even on issues of high consequence, stakeholders do their best to keep emotions and self-interests under wraps. Unfortunately for onlookers, this makes it even more difficult to gauge what vying individuals have at stake, the implications for the company in what's concluded, or the negative impact the vying might hold for any two-cohort or inter-unit relationship.

Time for an example, this one related by Mel, the CEO of a very successful start-up recently acquired by a New York Stock Exchange–listed conglomerate to be the flagship company of its space technology sector. A straight shooter by temperament, Mel was becoming increasingly frustrated by having to interact in a politicized environment reminiscent of the large companies he worked for prior to his start-up. Complaining about the daily politics entailed interacting with two executives he was only trying to help out. Here's how Mel described what he encountered:

Jim, the sector president to whom I report, called requesting I speak with David, the CEO of another company in our group. David's company manufactures parts similar to some of the components we use in the electronics we sell NASA. Apparently David has been complaining that we give no consideration to his company's bids in response to the RFQs [requests for quotations] we send out. Jim admonishes me for disloyalty and lack of team-play, to which I respond, "Where did you get that idea?

I'm not resisting David. Buying their components was never a consideration. We didn't buy from them before you acquired us, and we don't buy from them now. That's a fact."

Offline, I'm asking myself, "What in hell is Jim doing? He's not naïve. Both he and David know damn well why we don't consider their bids." So I tell Jim what he already knows: "Everything we build requires NASA certification. I'm not aware of any part produced in David's company even approaching NASA specs." I'm now thinking, "Jim is role-playing being the boss and testing me for obedience." Believing it best to keep my ego out of it, I decide to let Jim have his way. I tell Jim, "I'll call David immediately to figure out how I can give him some of the help he needs." Gratuitously, it seems to me, Jim responds, "That's the team spirit I'm looking for." Jim then gives me David's direct-line number. By this time I'm late for another meeting. I figure, given inter-coastal time differences, I'll call David first thing tomorrow morning.

Next day, about 10 a.m. my time, 1 p.m. David's, I place the call myself. Using the direct line reroutes me to the company's receptionist who, after saying my call is expected, instructs me to hold while she gets David. After a longer wait than I wanted, and having to listen to god-awful music, David's personal assistant clicks in saying, "It will be just five seconds more, David is finishing another call." She's off the line too fast for me to say, "How about his calling me back?"

Impatient and wanting to hang up, I waited while five seconds turned into five minutes and counting. I begin getting the idea that David is playing with me. Then David comes on the line with an offended-by-me attitude, which I decide to ignore. Referencing that I told Jim I'd call to help him out, I discover David was well aware of Jim admonishing me and miffed that I didn't call him immediately, as apparently Jim had told him I would.

Ignoring dealing with the new crime he's accusing me of, I graciously invite David out to see our manufacturing facilities and to discuss how our engineers might help his company upgrade to NASA standards."

Face-to-face, David owns up to the non-certification issue, and pleads ignorance to knowing the enhancements and testing required by NASA. Quickly I get the idea that David's been jerking Jim's chain, essentially blaming us for his company's inability to hit its numbers and grow. He wants our engineers to make the design changes his lack the ability to perform. This galls me, since we look to suppliers to help us upgrade our designs. Once again I reach for the off-switch on my ego, but it's getting harder to find.

Apparently the only idea David has for making his company profitable is selling components to us. Now I'm thinking, "What a jerk! I'm the only trick in his bag and he has the nerve to use Jim to intimidate me." I figure, "What the hell, so he's manipulative—what else is new in this world? I'll show him how a person with dignity behaves." So I offer to contribute $100,000 in engineering services to guide his people through the needed upgrades and the certification testing required by NASA. What's his response? Not a smile, just a perfunctory "thank you" that comes with an intonation that indicates I should be doing more. I tell him, "If you need more from us, we'll give it to you at our cost."

A week later I get an email, not a phone call, from Jim inviting me to a meeting identical to the one I just had with David. Adamant that I attend, he's insisting I fly cross-country to work out what David and I already concluded. As the email explains, Jim wants to give us his views on "sector company integration," which I interpret as an exercise in redundancy. I give him a call to ask, "What haven't we decided correctly?" And he can't name a thing. So I tell him, again, what I'm sure he knows from David: "We're on it. I just sent two top technical guys out to spend a month at David's company. Why not wait to see what they accomplish?" Making sure I'm out of this meeting I add, "Besides, I'm still post-surgical and busy as hell catching up after being out a month." I'm thinking to myself, "This is not the time to fly cross-country just so Jim can take credit by pretend-ing the progress we made was all his doing." But Jim doesn't give up. He tells me the meeting includes golf at a famous country club to which he belongs. Now I'm all but down to asking, "Do you want a doctor's note?" Instead, I just go quiet. Not giving up, Jim directs me to send my top-level manufacturing VP, adding, "We'll also include the engineers you've got working at David's company."

To me, the entire matter should be laughable, but I've allowed it to become a daily irritation. The only positive thing I accomplished was learning about Jim's intrusive-ness and my need to keep him off my back. From now on, I'm going to keep him out of as many loops as possible and remember to acknowledge his input for everything we achieve. What I can't figure out is what's between him and his corporate boss that he needs to take so much credit. It's a good thing I'm not younger because then I'd be irate. I've been around the barn too many times to be bogged down by time-wasting power plays like this. I made too much money in the company sale to put up with dumb stuff like this much longer.

Everyone Arrives with Scripts

This CEO's account illustrates the inevitability of in-company politics and the ease with which anyone can be drawn into playing a role in other people's dramas. Perturbed by the political dynamics he encountered, Mel realized he was too new to the scene to take any of the proceedings personally. He confided, "No doubt Jim and David were up to this prior to my showing up, and no doubt they'll be doing it after I leave."

Imperfect people with insecurities—read: all of us—come to work with scripts that re-create unreconciled dramas from their pasts. Unconsciously, they look for people to cast in feature roles, and settings in which to play the dramas out. Unfortunately, by the time people they cast catch on to what's transpiring, they're usually too involved to disengage, and stuck playing roles that lack meaningful payouts for them. Perhaps this describes the symbiotic element in Jim and David's relationship. It's a way of explaining Jim's need to assert himself with Mel, and David's attempt to hold Mel accountable for his company's missing sales.

Good Management Requires More than Extraordinary People

Like many, I have been fortunate to work with some personally evolved, and other-directed, empathetic leaders. Their managerial dealings reflected high degrees of intelligence, goodness, maturity, inner security, and honesty, and enough caring to understand how another person experiences a situation differently than themselves. At the time I worked with them, each had sufficient control of externalities to stay the course with their good behavior.

In fact, when discussing knotty management situations with clients and students, I frequently visualize a Mark, Gordon, Rossann, or Cliff to contemplate how one of them would deal with the issue puzzling the person seeking my advice. I think about the characteristic, quality, or manner of thinking these extraordinary managers might draw on. Then, when I next have an opportunity to speak with that individual, I inquire to see if I had their reasoning correct. In the process, I've identified a common orientation that gives some balance to self- and other-directed focusing. Faced with a good management behavior dilemma, I believe each of these individuals formulates, and gives full consideration to, three views of reality— the manager's (often their own), the petitioner's (the employee or lesser stature manager), and the company's (including the systems needed for producing good results). Each seems concerned with the well-being of each entity, and shuns problem formulations and solutions that allow only one or two of them to come out okay.

It's the Mentality That's Off

Unfortunately, there aren't enough extraordinary managers to go around. In fact, in one sense, having more would be a distraction. Receiving good management shouldn't hinge on finding the rare evolved manager to work for. There are more than enough smart, well-intentioned people who, with the right guidance and local culture supports, are fully capable of manifesting the other-directed, good management behavior that everyone needs to receive to be their best.

In case you need a reminder of how self-centered top-level managers can think and reason, and how absorption in their own accomplishments and success deprives people in their companies of focus, examine the note I received from Pete, the high-paid CEO of a three-thousand-plus-employee, highly profitable, publicly traded firm. I met Pete at a leadership award dinner where we were seated next to one another. Exchanging goodbyes, he asked for a signed copy of "the book you wrote lambasting performance reviews." In response to his receiving a copy and reading it, he wrote a gracious-sounding thank you.

But the note he wrote rubbed me wrong. Very wrong! To my eyes, it reflects the self-focused management mentality I want to see erased from Planet Earth. Take a look and see if you catch what I find so damaging and endemic in management thinking at the top.

Dear Dr. Culbert,

Thank you for sending me a copy of *Get Rid of the Performance Review!* which I had the pleasure of reading over the Thanksgiving break.

I found it (as you promised) thought provoking and often unfortunately amusing.

While I recognize so very many of the problems, systemic, and executional, which you accurately diagnose, I have been very fortunate to have benefited from well-designed and delivered reviews. At some point I would be pleased to chat with you about my personal experience.

An issue into which I continue to devote significant executive energy is trying to shape a coherent "Talent Ecosystem" which makes sense to colleagues and drives benefits to shareholders.

Once again, it was a pleasure to meet you and your wife in Los Angeles and hope that you had an enjoyable and peaceful Thanksgiving.

I hope our paths cross again.

With regards,
Pete[2]

Did you catch his self-directed focus and how it corrupts his good management thinking? Of course you spotted it. Unfortunately, Pete hasn't a clue. Does it bother you as much as it bothers me? *At his level, it's not supposed to be about him!* His assignment is staging for the effectiveness of the people performing work in his company, and to be ever on the lookout for ways to further their well-being. His job description does not stipulate self-infatuation and putting yourself above the pack. Why would his objective for a future discussion focus on additional bragging about his "personal experience"? He made it through the gauntlet, and has a peach of a job. But that job entails helping others get where they want to go, and removing obstacles and distractions from their paths. Talk about myopia! Compared to him, Mr. Magoo has 20/20 vision.

Are people like this CEO too gripped by the mind-set of accomplishing and realizing personal success to assume the management assignment of staging for others to accomplish and succeed on terms meaningful to them? I've met many executives like Pete and believe now is the time to give these people golden handshakes and the Winnebago they deserve.

Is Change Progress or Illusion?

When it's called to their attention, most managers quickly recognize the value of new management approaches and the importance of upgrading their current style. But the work culture has them fearful of taking a new direction and possibly making an image-discrediting mistake. Wading into the waters of change, but risking only one toe at a time, they seldom make sufficient headway to realize the momentum required to continue progressing. In the end, they talk enthusiastically about progressive practices but don't commit to system change. And do they ever talk. Knowing change is needed, wanting to think themselves avant-garde and progressive, they speak enlightenment words. But it's old wine in new bottles. Take a look at a sample of their new words.

Passing timelines and meeting benchmarks, managers "progress-up." They no longer make assignments, they provide "growth opportunities" and "challenge a person's potential." They don't ask for help, they "reach out." Their direct reports are no longer their employees, they are "business partners." They don't persuade and convince, they "discuss to get buy-in." They no longer assign people to project groups, they assign them to "tiger teams" and invite them to "take journeys together." Instead of working the data, it's a "deep dive" and "taking analysis to the next level." Finding someone proposing a course of action they like, they don't just concur, now they're "in *violent* agreement"—which always scares the hell out of me. When a manager wants someone's focus, they say "let me be honest with you" and "time to open the kimono" without realizing they might be admitting that past declarations lacked truthfulness and, should I say it, a certain degree of "intimacy." Do these words really change anything? Does anyone work "inside the box" anymore?!

The field of management has gone too many years implementing new and progressive management practices without much fundamental progress made. To me, what's going on is analogous to what takes place in the golf equipment industry. There's always a technological advancement that produces new and improved golf clubs that promise longer and more accurate shots. And the marketing works. Sales go up annually as golfers discard clubs they bought only a few years earlier to upgrade to more expensive high-tech clubs they expect will improve their game. And they're pleased because they do hit their balls farther and straighter. But their golf scores remain roughly the same. In the end, all they have to show for their purchase is their self-pride in having gone all out "to unleash their inner potential." Oh yes, they have great-looking, state-of-the-art, attractive clubs in the back of the golf carts they drive. Likewise, engaging in new progressive management practices isn't yielding appreciatively better scores.

Employees Don't Get What They Need from Managers

Employees want managers to perform their mandated other-directed duties. They need managers to help them accomplish what they're unable to do for themselves. But this entails managers acknowledging past insufficiencies, admitting error, and taking other-directed approaches to managing. Is it that managers need different guidance from their higher-level managers and leaders, or is it that they're too insecure and system suspicious to vary from what they know? Probably it's both.

Unfortunately, when managers find the approach they're using not working, too often their backup approach is going longer and stronger with the same approach that didn't work. And when that doesn't overpower employee resistance, you know what they do. It's a route we've already traveled. They blame their employee for not being responsive. Responsive to what? Responsive to the self-serving, pretentious practices the work culture claims is good managerial behavior.

When asking top-level managers how they got to the top, a large percentage cite someone "big" who, recognizing their potential, took them under their wing, so to speak, and set about opening doors. In today's lexicon that's called "being mentored." But I don't find mentoring a company plus. A mentor is someone playing favorites, short-circuiting the system, and ensuring preferential treatment at the expense of system-wide fair play.

Needless to say, mentors don't think what they're doing is negative. In their minds they're practicing good management, doing what's objectively right for the company. They're cultivating talent, keeping people challenged, and fast-tracking "high performers" to ensure the company doesn't lose them. It's as if what they are doing is part of some grand retention strategy. Well, as much as I hate to rain on anyone's happiness parade, playing favorites by mentoring is not the good management development system companies should be shooting for. Good management is not about mentoring one individual at a time. It's about fixing the system so that everyone can be their best and help the company, and creating the circumstances for individuals to realize their ambitions and dreams.

Conclusion

Managing in today's work culture is fraught with too many demands for managers to assume a more other-directed focus and mentality. To do so, managers would have to put self-pursuits on hold, drop the pretense of objectivity, and work collaboratively with cohorts to identify and remove obstacles to employee effectiveness companywide. Other-directed management requires providing employees the assurances needed to feel safe speaking their minds. Give employees a voice and managers will finally have the data they now lack for facing up to their mistakes and revising the erroneous reasoning that led to their making them. The way things are going now, what I'm talking about appears light-years away.

Under what circumstances can employees and cohorts expect to get the type of managerial good behavior they need? It's obvious; the culture has to change. Getting it changed is what I next address.

Notes

1. C. Argyris, "Skilled Incompetence," *Harvard Business Review* (September–October, 1986): 74–79.
2. First name signed in ink and changed to protect the guilty.

Part III

WHAT CAN BE DONE?

7

OVERCOMING CULTURAL RESISTANCE TO GOOD MANAGEMENT

It is only the oppressed who, by freeing themselves, can free the oppressors.

Paulo Freire[1]

You can talk improved practices, streamlined formats, and good managerial behavior until you're blue in the face, but given the way the work culture has managers thinking, I wouldn't count on anything substantial improving soon. There are just too many obstacles in the way of managers being up front about what they're doing. I'm convinced. I mean, just consider the response a manager might receive from cohorts, or a CEO, for saying, "How can we expect employees to speak candidly about their faults and limitations with us when we're not up front with one another about our own?"

I've never seen a shortage of good management ideas, or goodwilled people attempting company-wide improvements. But the work culture, call it the system, is always out there thwarting progress, and making it difficult for any progressive initiative to endure after its sponsors leave the scene. The system is far more constraining than what's apparent. Given the efforts and money spent educating, training, and coaching managers, and the tremendous commitment of managerial time devoted to such efforts, I find the return on investment miniscule.

Let's be clear: there have been many bright moments at individual companies. Look what Bernie Marcus and Arthur Blank achieved cloning managers and using fail-safe computerized inventory and ordering systems. In an amazingly short period of time, they took Home Depot from start-up to industry leader.[2] How about Louis Gerstner's personal assault on the cultural corruption he encountered taking over at IBM, and the turnaround business model he insisted IBM partners use.[3] Then there's the storied management problems Starbucks suffered when founder Howard Schultz retired, and the risk-taking initiatives he unleashed rebirthing himself as CEO.[4] And look what Elon Musk is accomplishing with new venture companies the likes of Tesla and SpaceX. What's his secret? Inspirational projects, apparently: he's known as hands-on all the way. Strong-willed leaders with enlightened inner compasses can accomplish a great deal asserting what they think is needed, and insisting people either get with their program or get out of the way.

I was ever so impressed when Apple CEO Tim Cook announced his gay identity.[5] Surfing the waves of a record sales quarter, he leveraged his stature to create a new level of acceptance for diversity of any kind in his company, with spillovers at other firms. I see his coming out leading to a baseline mentality and sensibility that people in every company deserve. But apparently it wasn't an action just any Apple executive felt safe initiating. Tim Cook himself didn't for his first sixteen years at Apple—and he was CEO for three of those!

On Culture Change

Unfortunately for the world of work, culture changes very slowly, and good management is needed today. Waiting for cultural change to make good management happen will not get your company much relief. Look at the gun culture in our country. Everyone, even bona fide National Rifle Association cardholders, realize change is needed. But none occurs.

I was sure change was on the way when the Brady Act was passed, even though it took twelve years of congressional hearings to get a vote. But no substantial change followed its passing. And how about the public outcries after each new headline shooting: Columbine High School in 1999; Gabby Giffords's speech in 2011; Sandy Hook Elementary School in 2012; Fort Hood in 2014—and I haven't gotten to Mother Emanuel or San Bernardino or the Pulse Nightclub massacre, not to mention the other senseless acts of violence that will undoubtedly take place before and after this book is published. Everyone knows things are off. Yet I've seen no change of real consequence in my lifetime, and I doubt my children will see much change in theirs. That's the way with culture. I could say the same thing about MBA education and performance reviews—come to think of it, I have.

Failed Attempts at Work-Culture Change

I've participated in two global consortiums established for affecting work-culture change. Each involved many thousands of professionals innovating and implementing progressive work practices based on assumptions very different from the ones responsible for much of the bad management behavior one sees today. One consortium began in the late 1940s, the other about a decade later. Dissimilar in approaches, their goals and underlying assumptions aligned. Both had strong academic roots and many participants from industry. And by the time I joined in, each was a gathering force of progressiveness in the workplace, and society more broadly. While remnants of consortium-promoted practices exist in companies today, and research continues to be performed, neither consortium developed sufficient mass to have its precepts embedded in a mainstream way. Today they serve as background tapestry that leaders looking to promote progressiveness in their firms can draw upon for guidance.

Both consortiums were composed of activist scientists, interventionist practitioners, and industrial and societal leaders dedicated to helping people live increasingly potentiated and productive lives at work. Each envisioned a workplace characterized by fair play, transparency, self-determination, and governance that ensured a voice for all participants, and held everyone accountable, managers included, for how their actions impacted the productivity of other individuals and work units. None of this was intended to usurp formal lines of authority; everything was aimed at removing barriers to enterprise-wide cooperation.

Although it was seldom referred to as such, I'm calling the first consortium Applied Humanistic Psychology. Embodying the humanistic tenets of what social scientists refer to as the "third force" in psychology, this consortium promoted managerial self-awareness, sensitivity to others, social consciousness, and the increasing emancipation of individuals.

The second consortium was called Socio-Technical Systems and Design (STS) in academia and Quality of Working Life (QWL) in industry, and, eventually, in every type of organization. As the first label suggests, this consortium focused on redesigning work systems to align the technology of production with the character of the people performing work. It sought ways of restructuring work activities based on how employees could best contribute individually, and collectively working in groups.

Centers of gravity in diverse academic disciplines—the first in psychology, the second in engineering and technology—both consortiums were considered value-driven, applied sciences. The core investigative method for each was theory-directed intervention in real-time work situations, with rigorous documentation of impact. The standard experimental procedure was: 1) Conceive a theoretically based, situationally appropriate, workplace intervention and implement it;

2) Collect data to assess the effects and impact of the methodology applied; 3) Analyze the data for relevance to modifying theory, and refine the intervention plan accordingly; 4) Intervene again and collect more data; and 5) Use the data to validate the theory and, if results fall short of goals, make data-directed changes and repeat the process. Hence the name "action research."

Attending conferences, reading journals, and engaging in a good deal of networking, at no time was I aware of either consortium encountering strenuous resistance, notwithstanding occasional projects being blocked due to opposition within specific companies. Taken in total, each consortium had long runs of success. The Applied Humanistic Psychology consortium spawned a new professional discipline called Organization Development (OD), with thousands of companies employing cadres of discipline-schooled professionals. These professionals convened interpersonal-effectiveness workshops, facilitated off-site team-building discussions, women's support groups, and Black-White Awareness programs. There were similar pedagogy-based courses in hundreds of universities. Sensitivity training, T-groups (or training groups), ropes courses, EST training, et cetera, were wildly popular in society at large. There was a sensation-creating article on T-groups in industry published in the then mainstream *Look* magazine—a cover story exclaiming "It's OK to Cry at the Office."[6]

The Quality of Working Life/Socio-Tech Systems consortium instigated autonomous functioning work groups, hands-off management, and production cost-cutting processes now used in high-profile large companies such as Volvo, DuPont, Alcoa, and Procter & Gamble. It was responsible for innovative worker participation in designing production processes for Toyota and Saturn. Its precepts underlie the much publicized Lockheed Martin Skunk Works, where the F-117 stealth fighter plane was designed and built in breakneck speed. While I've only scratched the surface, I'm guessing much of what I'm talking about is news to you. Herein lies the problem.

You would have heard about all of this had these innovative work practices become mainstream in the culture at large.

Cultural Resistance to Change

I now liken trying to change what the culture has wrong to what someone out to eradicate a computer virus encounters. Sensing detection, the virus activates an algorithm aimed at resisting the extraction being applied. I see many work-culture-change-resistant algorithms today. Most immediately, I see a very effective semantic algorithm that resists people questioning status quo practices, never mind holding the dialogue needed in order to conceive what should change.

The resisting algorithm to which I'm referring stipulates: "Don't waste valuable time bringing up problems for which no solutions are known." This makes it difficult to address culturally caused troublesome situations one doesn't yet understand sufficiently well to fix—that is, without appearing to engage in what the work culture stigmatizes as a *time-wasting* endeavor. Constrained by the illogic of this algorithm, and lacking practical solutions, those coping with incoherent situations hit a wall; not only do issues become very difficult to view, they become almost impossible to discuss.

Too much of what the culture expects flies below most managers' consciousness—vaguely recognized, not engaged, and kept in place because managers are hard-pressed to identify how they're being influenced. You want specifics? Try these—discussed in this book: employees not being able to speak candidly about what they need and are not receiving from their manager (described in chapter 2); managers worrying so much about their image that they forget what they know that is correct (described in chapter 3); top-tier managers who won't tell the CEO there's something wrong in his or her thinking (*LA Times* DTO story, also in chapter 3); reports not being able to speak candidly about company effectiveness problems with managers who have the authority to fix them (several stories in chapter 1); the punishments meted out to people who stand accountable to the extent that no one wants to step up and say, "I did it" (discussion of accountability in chapter 2); managers forced to compete with employees in taking credit for workplace accomplishments (rising tide discussion in chapter 2). I could go on—and now will.

Differentiating Leadership from Management

Another difficulty managers have in facing up to their bad behavior stems from the work culture's failure to distinguish between *leading* and *managing*. People holding executive titles such as CEO, president, vice president, and director are expected to be leaders—a role that is often portrayed as big-picture focused, and employee directive. It's their job to stipulate and oversee the course of the company—each unit and each function—and stand accountable for bottom-line results. It's appropriate for them to issue directives and insist people follow their lead. To this end they direct, deploy, delegate, decide, and pass judgments as they see the need. After all, when results are tabulated, they receive credit for what's accomplished and fault for what is not. There's no way around the fact that it was either their plan, or the one they agreed to, and their responsibility to ensure that operatives coordinated and teamed up. They determined the budget dedicated for each function. They were responsible for choosing the right people, and it's the authority they delegated that managers below them used in deploying people and giving out assignments. Success or disappointment, the responsibility for company results is theirs.

People holding leadership titles are also expected to stipulate the mentality used in managing employees. They're charged with getting the overall system arranged to facilitate everyone's effectiveness. They determine the practices and protocols that all operatives and managers must use. When leading, they're supposed to keep the big picture in focus to ensure the company maintains a strategic course.

On a daily basis, however, most leaders spend their time tactically—solving problems, checking up on individuals and operations, and getting themselves informed. They also have direct reports to *manage*, mostly managers and a few staff functionaries, and these people expect an inquiring, other-directed focus. But, especially in large companies, this is not what most people receive from leaders. Accustomed to giving directives, most leaders are inclined to treat direct reports as extensions of themselves.

Like leaders, managers have implementation decisions to make, and for these a self-asserting focus is appropriate. But this is only part of their assignment. Much more of their time is supposed to be spent in other-directed pursuits—coaching and supporting direct reports, and helping them accomplish, develop, and succeed. This entails sizing up people for their skill sets, inclinations, and limitations, and making individual-appropriate assignments. Managers also have a more ethereal responsibility: helping people accomplish, get recognition, and make progress toward their goals.

Good managing entails giving people some latitude in figuring things out. It entails inquiring about how people see situations and their inclinations to act, and discussing how individuals can best go about accomplishing for the company and themselves. Good managers give operatives up-front information about the resources and budgets they are authorized to draw upon, and are explicit about the limits of authority being delegated. They seek to build trusting relationships that permit candid give-and-take on any issue that arises, whether it be operational or stylistic. In every instance, good management behavior begins with a question, not a declarative.

Where's the Incentive for Other-Directed Managing?

Most managers believe they know what's required for good results and find telling people what to do far more efficient than explaining what's needed and then getting into their "heads." It takes time to inquire, guide, coach, and support— what the textbooks claim to be desirable, other-directed, good managerial behavior. Moreover, many managers become anxious when the people whose operations they depend on work independently of their influence. They fear that some action or decision they don't know about will jeopardize work-unit results, depriving them of the credit they seek.

How much of an other-directed focus to assume when managing is both a matter of inclination and circumstance. Inclination depends on such factors as a manager's need for control and unique chemistry with an individual. But regardless of circumstance and chemistry, what people holding leadership and manager titles need implanted in their thinking is that leading and managing are distinct activities and the company needs both to take place. Self-directed is for managing resources and systems. Other-directed is for staging people to work independently and accomplish on their own. The managerial inputs are quite different. Each activity requires a different focus and use of self.

The distinction between self-directed, individual contributions and other-directed activities occurs to me each time an executive approaches me with an offer to teach a course at the Anderson School. The personal circumstances cited are usually fairly similar. The executive says something like: "I've made more money than I'll ever need. I don't want to just retire, and I'd like to remain societally productive. There's a great deal I'd like to pass on."

While their sincerity and generosity of spirit are seldom in doubt, what these executives have to offer is not what I see MBA students needing. I ask, "What do you teach students after describing how you did it, what you knew, and what you learned after that? Of course students will gain from knowing how you operated and what made you a success. But each student has different skills, interests, ambitions, and aptitudes, and the situations they face are never the same as the ones in which you succeeded. In each instance they need to self-assess and find their own best ways of doing things." Then, to break the tension, I smile and say something like, "Besides, I don't want you taking my job." Usually they get the message and agree.

The good management mandate stipulates managers be other-supportive team players, and willing to help others accomplish and realize their ambitions for doing so. Good-behaving managers don't compete for recognition with direct reports, or act stealthily with cohorts. The mandate stipulates open communications, which means establishing sufficient trust for employees to speak their truths without fearing negative consequences. Good-behaving managers don't withhold information, engage in backroom politics, or conduct themselves in ways that cause cohorts to feel insecure.

The inability to distinguish between leading, managing, and working on one's own produces management assumptions I find devoid of common sense. It's ridiculous to think that *anyone* can manage. It's naïve to assume that no one complaining indicates good management behavior is taking place. Get realistic. Some people are just too self-focused or insecure to get another person very straight. People like this have no business being allowed to assign anyone a parking space, let alone determine someone's in-company fate. Besides, direct reports wanting to get good ratings and keep their jobs don't challenge their manager, or complain to their manager's boss.

If you're inclined to be taken in by such empty ideas, then you're likely to find what I have to say next breaking news. There is no single "best" management style. Each manager crafts a style to emphasize what they believe is them at their very best, and then has to adjust it for each direct report's unique penchants and needs. What's more, by virtue of personal temperament, people with manager titles put different amounts of effort into other-directedness—regardless of how they've been instructed or trained.

There's a relatively simple way to determine a person's inclination to manage. Ask the individual what they're out to accomplish, what they're doing to accomplish it, and why they decided to go about it the way they did. If the person answers with activities leading to company-needed results, it's likely their natural inclination is self-directed. If the person answers with a process aimed at facilitating other people accomplishing, you may, in fact, have evidence of a good management mentality. But don't conclude "always" from a single inquiry. More might be taking place in the moment, so it's best to ask a few times prior to concluding.

Companies need both leadership and management. Top-level managers need to know what their company has, and decide whether they've got, the needed mix. If, as I've been contending, leaders believe employees need more other-directedness, then it's up to them to come up with a change-management process and provide incentives for managers engaging in that process.

Preparing a Company for Culture Change

I don't see the culture at large changing until leaders in some number of high-profile companies actively promote thinking that corrects for what the workplace erroneously expects. Theory and logical arguments won't make it happen—my consortium experiences have me convinced of that. Shifting social values are always an iffy proposition. Lagging workplace equity for women and minorities, and gun-owner-rights blockages of legislation, have shown me it takes a lot more than golden-rule values and practical common sense.

The good news is that individual companies don't have to wait for the culture at large to change to realize the benefits of other-directed management behavior, authenticity, and real team-play camaraderie. Company leaders have the means to get the management mentality they want. But it takes a valid process and a great deal of earnest commitment at the top level to get it done.[7]

If You Want Change, You Must Unlock the Past

Teaming up with company leaders, I've participated in dozens of change-management initiatives and have read accounts of many more. Most were begun in a way I used to find reasonable, and now see as intrinsically flawed. They began with statements of enthusiasm and, I wish I could say this differently, a big-pitch sales job that emphasized all the positives. For years I didn't give this positive-thinking approach a second thought. But reflecting on the causes of some stalled implementations, and interviewing less than enthusiastic participants, I eventually realized the big flaw in this approach.

No matter how valid and effective the new behavior called for, it's unrealistic to expect a one-step, "here's an irresistibly good idea, now implement it" mandated shift in mind-set and behavior. That's not how people inwardly work. Change requires more than convincing people of the advantages in doing things differently; it also requires people releasing from the mind-sets that justified the behavior the new initiative is asking them to replace.

So now when advising leaders on change-management initiatives, I urge giving explicit attention to assisting people to, my words, *unlock themselves from the past*. I recommend expanding the standard communication roll-out message from "Here's what we want and the benefits we expect" to additionally include some version of "Here are the erroneous assumptions we've been making, and here's what we overlooked and ignored that allowed us to go so long missing what now appears obviously wrong, and not searching for better ways to proceed."

Why insist on so much humble pie? Because people are being asked to change more than behavior. They are also being asked to release from a thought process that accounted for behavior they're now being told is so wrong that it needs immediate replacing. Mental speed bumps are involved that they'll have to negotiate them on their own. Why not give them some support!

I find it both courageous and smart when, after stipulating new desirables, leaders take steps to correct, counter, quarantine, and, may I go so far as to use the term *exorcize*, the erroneous thinking that caused the previous way of proceeding to make sense. *Courageous* because doing so acknowledges human fallibility and provides tacit permission for questioning other company practices. *Smart* because exposing the flawed logic serves as a counterforce to people reverting to what's more practiced and familiar, especially when under pressure. An example of such a back-sliding took place at Apple when, in the year 2000, enlightened HR leaders mandated an immediate cessation of performance reviews. Unfortunately, and to make my point, they did so without holding a thorough debunking discussion. It took but five years for managers in over half the work units to reinstate reviews, with some initiating additional schemes for grading employees and with no consistency company-wide.[8]

What I'm describing is similar to what's off when consulting companies contract to review some organization practice, or operational unit, for the purposes of suggesting improvements, or even to come up with an entire strategic plan. While the substance of what's reported is usually clarifying and accurate, and suggested recommendations valuable ones to make, too seldom does anything durable get implemented. Why not? Because few consultant reports include a list of the forces resisting implementation, and a plan for overcoming them. Consulting companies sell optimism. It's not in their interests to identify resistance, or get involved in helping managers surmount it. They might fail.

Company leaders wanting change need processes that expose the flawed managerial thinking that went into coming up with practices they would now like to replace. The logic for the good-behavior thinking they are now requesting is usually apparent, even obvious. What's not obvious are the cultural assumptions and expectations that underlie how managers were previously indoctrinated. No surprises here. Erroneous thinking was in the water everyone was given to drink. The effects don't spontaneously dissipate upon leaders stipulating something better.

Cultural Expectations That Need Replacing

I'd now like to contribute a starter list of five culture-at-large expectations that need explicit airing and revising. I do this in the spirit of helping leaders disabuse managers of what they falsely believe that resists their assuming more of an other-directed focus. Of course, there are many other expectations that leaders should disabuse, and each of the five I list require company-specific elaborations.

1. Cultural Expectation for Immediate Accomplishment

Let's start with the short-term "what have you done for me today" *immediate accomplishment* mentality that the work culture propounds, and people expect to meet. Constructively, it connects inputs to outputs and makes it difficult for people to avoid standing accountable for time spent performing activities that don't yield productive results. Unfortunately, it also serves as a counterforce to other-directed managerial behavior.

The immediate-accomplishment expectation creates an unrelenting pressure for corporate executives and business unit leaders to keep their company on course in meeting quarterly forecasted goals—sometimes in pennies per share of earnings. But meeting this expectation has downsides, and people need to be aware of them. It causes leaders to focus on the immediate and forego actions that could lead to big-gain payoffs in the longer term. It can cause CEOs to sell off valuable undeveloped company assets. Why would they want to do that? For a couple of reasons. First, it gets the company's EBITDA (earnings before interest, taxes, depreciation, and amortization) up. But there's an even more self-serving reason: many CEOs have their bonuses tied to this metric. That's how I read the motivation for the *LA Times* fiasco (described in chapter 3). Why else would a new CEO tinker with something as inflammatory as employee time off and vacation?

This expectation is almost always a negative when it comes to the management of people. It's a source of disorientation that leads some managers to see the sensitive human beings reporting to them as "human assets," and to monetize their every contribution. It's the motive behind hierarchical relationships and managers' satisfaction with one-sided accountability. It's in the fabric that prevents employees and managers speaking forthrightly to people who can influence their fates.

The immediate-accomplishment expectation leads to some managers thinking that all that's needed to get the employee behavior they desire, which they aren't getting now, is to state their displeasure and then stand back to watch while the employee instantly changes. That's not the way to stage for someone's development. Even a smart guide dog can't reorient that fast. But it is a sure-fire way to get employees to hide what they think a manager faults, and to fake competence, mastery, and acquiescence.

Good management behavior is other-directed and long-term developmental. It entails a manager making inputs contoured for appropriateness to another person's thought processes and then allowing sufficient time for that person to decide for themselves the means of improving what they can. Good management begins with a question, not a stipulation. This is why I've long endorsed skin-in-the-game accountability, where the manager's accomplishments are reified in the success of their employees. That's what management is supposed to be about. I don't know better metrics for measuring good management than direct reports' accomplishments, feelings of personal success, and trust level with the manager. Not practical? Well, it's something to think about.

2. Cultural Expectation for Objectivity

Next is the unrealistic view of human nature that the work culture promulgates by expecting managers to be objective, despite there being no leader or manager—or any human being, for that matter—in possession of such capabilities. Meeting this expectation requires massive amounts of pretense—and this leads to feelings of self-alienation, insensitivity to others, and inauthentic, suspicion-arousing behavior. It blocks people from identifying the bases for their differing viewpoints and holding an honest, open-minded discussion to reconcile viewpoints and disagreements. Obvious limitations—something more is needed.

Now let me refer you to a fact that's often overlooked when people pretend objectivity is possible. The presence of subjectivity, bias, and self-interested pursuits does not preclude genuine concern and respect for others, or helping employees advance important self-interested agendas. Everyone knows self-interests are omnipresent, and few people resent others getting what they want, particularly if they're acknowledged for the help and acceptance they lend. In fact, sincere concern for the interests of direct reports, cohorts, and other work units is the core goodwill activity in other-directed management.

I instruct MBA students that most interpersonal transactions involve three distinct sets of interests—one's own, the other person's, and the two-party relationship taken as an entity in and of its own. Each needs to be respected and nurtured as it's possible. Why respected? Because none of these three are going away as long as you and the other person have dealings, so it's best to keep each entity viable. Don't neglect your own interests; self-interests are the reason you took your job. Look out for the other person's and you'll get the benefits of their reciprocation. Ignore someone's needs and your neglect will never be forgotten. Take care of the relationship; it's the vehicle for getting more things accomplished.

Of course, there's always a fourth consideration: the interests of the company. Make the company prosperous and everyone is better off. However, what the company needs is subject to self-interested interpretation. No matter who you're working with, that will always require discussion.

3. Cultural Expectation of Accountability

Everyone understands that accountability is an empty construct unless consequences follow misbehavior. An acknowledgment of responsibility for a mistake or bad result is mere words without assurance that a consequence will take place.

However, when people think about consequences there's only one word that comes to most people's mind. That word is *punishment*—often in the form of rewards denied. Without a punishment, there's no accountability. In a company there are many ways to be punished (or deprived of rewards): pay, advancement, assignment, et cetera. Unfortunately, stakes like these serve as disincentives to people owning up. Why doesn't the world of work get that? People never abandon self-interests. When punishment is assured, people avoid standing accountable.

But there's another way to extract accountability. It's too bad more people don't think of it. Consequences, yes! In addition to punishment, can you think of some other way to hold someone accountable?

Take a moment. See if you can.

There's a way of extracting accountability that most people consider preferable—once they envision it. I'm referring to *lessons-learned accountability.* Did the person turning in the disappointing performance learn sufficiently from their experience to provide the people depending on their good performance reason to believe similar issues won't occur again? If the individual learned enough about the erroneous or shortsighted thinking that caused their actions, then everyone is better off.

It's not lessons-learned accountability when someone merely concludes, "I'll never get caught doing that again," or some variation. If that's all that's learned then no one is better off. Something much more substantive needs to be realized, or that individual remains a ticking time bomb—ready to detonate when another like circumstance occurs. Assumptions and motivations need to be probed, and blind spots preventing the person recognizing their difficulties need to be faced, essential skills acquired, and remedies assured. What's realized must be substantial.

I've long been a proponent of two-sided accountability—hold the operative accountable for results, and that person's manager accountable for providing what was needed for the operative to deliver good results.[9] Thus, any time an operative makes an error material enough to be held accountable, it's appropriate for the operative's manager to also stand accountable. How? By learning what was needed, and not provided in sufficient depth, in the service of preventing similar-issue disappointments. In the process, two imperfect people learn more, and the company benefits. Moreover, what the manager learns can be leveraged to dealings with other reports and operatives. What if the manager doesn't learn enough? Then you have an indication that his or her boss needs to learn a few things as well.

4. Cultural Expectation of Perfection

People are imperfect, but the work culture doesn't accept this. Why not? Because imperfect people can be expected to err, and the culture at large is intolerant of mistakes. How much does the work culture dislike mistakes? To the point of making it very difficult for people needing help to own up to what they don't know, and seek additional resources prior to screwing up. For example, four years into his presidency, George W. Bush was asked at a news conference about the biggest mistake he had made since 9/11; he would not admit to one.[10]

Likewise, it took until after his second election for President Barack Obama, now lame duck with nothing to lose, to admit to lessons learned, and to verbalize how he should have gone about his presidency differently.[11]

And look at the widespread use of performance reviews that assume everyone can become excellent on almost any metric used to judge them. That practice denies that imperfect people succeed in different ways—using the skills they have and avoiding skills they lack. Performance reviews equate to a manager–direct report power game with the manager taking all the power by engaging in an activity that denies there's any bias in their scoring of people. Think about it. You've got a flawed person with more power alleging he or she can accurately assess the strengths and flaws of a person with less power, with the less powerful individual fearful of contesting what they see falsely alleged—concerned that if they do, they'll be faulted for being defensive. And no one is reading that person a Miranda.

The cultural expectation of perfection makes it difficult for people to be open about their needs to learn. Any "uninformed" question on a topic of some presumed area of competency can get interpreted as an admission of deficiency. But companies want people owning up to gaps in understanding, and seeking assistance as they have the need. It's always better to have someone ask a stupid question now than to make a dumb mistake later. Everyone recognizes the company loses out when people hide errors and deny mistakes. Not nearly as many recognize that everyone loses out when people have to pretend they know more than they do, which, to be convincing, often extends to people pretending to themselves as well as others.

Perhaps the biggest damage perpetrated by the *expectation of perfection* is the obstacle it creates to people bringing their authentic selves to work. I've often contended the most effective and efficient management tool is a trusting relationship, with authenticity as the core ingredient. Authenticity takes people to interpersonal places competency alone will never reach. People are imperfect; getting better is a lifelong pursuit. Saying "I don't know" is the first step on anyone's path to learning.

5. Cultural Expectation of Competitiveness

Go to any organization of size, ask managers about teamwork, and probably every answer you get will emphasize its importance. Now sit back and listen to what people say about working with other units, and observe their interactions relating to people in those units. Most likely you'll hear all the right words, but I doubt you'll see nearly as much cooperation as what people profess. Despite the ever-present pretense of team-play, cooperation, and goodwill, I find a good deal of what takes place between work units in large companies *ethnocentric competition*.

The competition should be with marketplace competitors, not between cohorts vying for viewpoint or jurisdictional dominance. But too often it's work-unit parochialism and jurisdictional boundaries that dictate managerial allegiances, not overall company well-being. I find this thinking exemplified when people refer to a "silo mentality" in characterizing the lack of data-sharing and joint-effort problem-solving in their company. It bespeaks of cohort competition and who benefits from workplace accomplishments. Not once have I heard the term "silo" inside a startup, ESOP (employee stock ownership plan), or any *do-good* organization where people are out to improve the world.

Until what's actually transpiring is acknowledged, and drivers of internal competition identified and addressed, teamwork problems will continue despite all cooperation alleged. That's why I eschew discretionary bonuses. If the team does a good job, why pick apart who contributed what, and which contributions were most valuable. Let everyone enjoy a fair portion of the gratitude distributed.

Conclusion

Leaders wanting other-directed good management in their companies can get it done on their own. Believing they might need some help in doing so, I've changed my approach. In addition to raising awareness and adding perspective, I've begun offering advice. There's a great deal in what the culture at large expects that needs to be revised.

Breaking out from erroneous expectations is a big part. Also needed are destinations to head toward and processes for getting there. To contribute, I've got a revealing case study to tell you about, and specific suggestions for destinations. That's what I write about next.

Notes

1. P. Freire, *Pedagogy of the Oppressed* (New York: Seabury, 1970).
2. B. Marcus and A. Blank, *Built From Scratch* (New York: Crown, 1999).
3. L.V. Gerstner, *Who Says Elephants Can't Dance?* (New York: Harper, 2002).
4. H. Schultz, *Onward: How Starbucks Fought for Its Life without Losing Its Soul* (New York: Rodale, 2011).
5. Timothy Donald Cook, "Tim Cook Speaks Up," Bloomberg Technology, October 30, 2014. http://www.bloomberg.com/news/articles/2014-10-30/tim-cook-speaks-up
6. J. Poppy, "It's OK to Cry at the Office," *Look*, July 9, 1968.
7. Arguments similar to mine have been made by several theorists and researchers. For those interested in pursuing this line of reasoning, I can recommend books that I've found quite informative: T.E. Deal and A.A. Kennedy, *Corporate Cultures: The Rites and Rituals of Corporate Life* (Reading, MA: Addison Wesley, 1982); L.G. Bolman and T.E. Deal, *Reframing Organizations: Artistry, Choice and Leadership* (San Francisco: Jossey-Bass Inc., 1997); E. Schien, *Organizational Culture and Leadership*, 4th ed (San Francisco: Jossey-Bass, 2010); and, most recently, L.G. Bolman and T.E. Deal, *How Great Leaders Think: The Art of Reframing* (San Francisco: Jossey-Bass, 2014).
8. Related to me by Dan Miller, Apple's chief talent officer, in 2000.

9. For more on these ideas see S.A. Culbert and J.B. Ullmen, *Don't Kill the Bosses!* (San Francisco: Berrett-Kohler, 2004).

10. Asked by John Dickerson of *Time* magazine, reported in the University of California American Presidency Project, April 13, 2004.

11. Interview on *Charlie Rose*, reported by John Dickerson in *Slate*, July 13, 2012. http://www.slate.com/articles/news_and_politics/politics/2012/07/barack_obama_told_charlie_rose_he_had_made_mistakes_but_it_was_really_a_humblebrag_.html

8

GETTING COMPANY SUPPORTS FOR GOOD MANAGEMENT

Lamenting the difficulties managers have reifying their good intentions, I've taken readers on an excursion through the force field that throws managers off—and the ensuing dynamics that have them constantly on edge. I did so believing it's time people understand why so much managerial misbehaving takes place. I described the daily preoccupations that prevent managers from assuming an other-directed focus. I wanted employees to realize that most of the neglect and insensitivity they receive is performed with no malice intended. It's largely the result of managers dealing with small crises of their own.

I wanted managers to become more aware of the sources of their constant distraction, and the hollowness of the rationales they use to soothe and reassure themselves. I believed many would see my analysis useful in finding a path that brings them closer to their good management goals. I hoped my explanations would prove a useful perspective to managers reconsidering the priorities they live.

Very important, I wanted to make company leaders, CEOs, and top-tier managers with leadership responsibilities aware of the ever-present concerns distracting the people they count on to implement their plans. As managers of managers, it's their job to decide the type of managerial mentality they want in their company, and to install processes that put managers on a course to acquiring it. There's no question in my mind that much of what today's work culture considers good management behavior lessens the effectiveness of everyone in the chain.

Having said this, I'm aware that we're at a point where readers want to know if there's a fix, and, if there is, what's involved and who has what role in delivering it? Keep in mind we're talking about much more than replacing a protocol or modifying an established practice. We're talking about overriding cultural programming, changing mind-sets, and installing processes aimed at getting managers to evolve their thinking.

What's Involved in Managers Breaking Out?

Breaking out of today's status quo requires leaders committed to insisting managers' mentalities evolve. I've observed and facilitated many change-management initiatives and have concluded company leaders are the only ones positioned to insist and get this done. I'm not talking about the annual all-hands meeting where the CEO and an assortment of leaders take turns at the podium speaking big-picture abstractions and feel-good platitudes. And it isn't an assignment that can be delegated to HR professionals, or outsourced to consultants. Evolving a company's management thinking requires top-tier leaders to stipulate objectives and install processes that force managers out of culturally conforming comfort zones. It also entails providing supports and rewards for managers doing so.

Required are leaders convinced that an evolved managerial mentality will augment their company's bottom line. This is not to say that's all they believe it takes to get good results, or that increased profitability is the only benefit good management behavior will yield. But believing bottom-line benefits follow from evolved managerial thinking is essential to leaders persevering when other exigencies compete for their attention. And exigencies always arise.

Company initiatives aimed at changing how managers view situations and interact are always being attempted. Some leaders have insisted upon enormous changes in managerial reasoning, and many of those were accomplished.[1] In fact, I haven't heard an account of a CEO-led initiative failing when top-tier leaders stood shoulder to shoulder insisting managers get it done. But it takes committed leaders, and a committed CEO's involvement.

Considerable discussion is needed for people leading a change-management initiative to agree on the shifts in mentality they want. Starting out, they know they have differences, but it takes a while to learn just how significant seemingly small differences can be. In my experience, there's no real agreement or binding commitment until group members fully divulge the personal bases for what they individually assert is essential for good management.

After stipulating a mentality, leaders need to install processes aimed at moving managers closer to the reasoning they want. For example, if they want more other-directedness, they need to make it in a manager's self-interest to acquire mindsets supporting that focus. They might establish incentives—rewards and bribes. They might specify specific behaviors and the frequency of their occurrence, with disincentives for failures to perform as requested—penalties and punishments. Far better, they will provide self-motivational processes that allow managers to experience the benefits of an other-directed focus and find their own ways to embrace it. In a moment I'll relate a case study that illustrates the process I'm out to describe.

What needs to take place is much easier to achieve in small companies. It's far more difficult to accomplish in large organizations where people feel the need to defend past decisions and current courses of action. In either instance, I find CEO buy-in required. Louis Gerstner[2] described how he got every top-level IBM manager's commitment to the mind-set he was insisting upon after threatening that any hesitation adopting it would cost managers their job. Successful as he was, with that kind of gun-to-the-head approach one should never be confident that people are telling you their true beliefs. Years earlier, "Chainsaw" Al Dunlap made saber-rattling declarations similar to Gerstner's at Scott Paper, and his reputation preceded him when he took over Sunbeam.[3] Word out about his ruthless treatment of employees at Scott, droves of essential employees told Dunlap they'd be loyal—up until the moment they found jobs elsewhere and quit.

Case Study

Relevant to this discussion is my five years of consulting on a change-in-mentality initiative in a 150,000-employee, high-profile, multinational company. It's a company that spends a gazillion dollars annually on management training and quality-of-work-life enhancements. Even taking into account what I saw in the consortium eras at Procter & Gamble in the '70s and '80s, I know of no company whose leaders put more time and energy into establishing an employee-sensitive, consumer-considerate, and societally-contributing management mentality.

> My assignment began when several top-level managers with company-wide leadership responsibilities, including the senior HR person, called on me to help them sort through their ambivalences about the company's reliance on performance reviews.
> Decision made to eliminate reviews, I was retained to advise them on matters related to getting rid of reviews and using the absence of them as a means of improving company-wide management.

The initial step entailed getting interconnected systems decoupled from the scores people received on reviews. Up until this point, reviews had been instrumental in determining pay, bonuses, stock options, and career advancement opportunities. I had several pieces of advice: "Pay for the job, not the performance"; "Award bonuses based on work-unit results, not individual efforts"; and "Let everyone in the work-unit team share—either the same amount or the same percent of their salary. Likewise for stock options." I didn't want people working together competing for any kind of recognition or remuneration. My rationale: remove any reason people might have to not cooperate with someone needing their assistance. In fact, provide an incentive for being a helpful, considerate teammate. Make sure people working together win together.

As for career advancement and promotion, I recommended open bidding and hiring panels led by the recruiting boss. I advised, "Wherever possible, exclude current bosses." Jobs would be posted, people could self-assess and apply, panelists would conduct interviews and later discuss and compare. But in the end, there would be no vote, just an exchange of opinions. The recruiting boss would make the selection.

I figured, you can debate individual attributes all you want, but there's no objective way to determine who's going to do the best job. What could be accomplished, however, was holding the recruiting boss accountable for the success of whomever he or she selected. Let the recruiting boss choose the individual they felt could best help their unit. Then hold that boss accountable for the selected person's results.

More generally, I recommended excluding the current boss's input to remove a possible disincentive for direct reports speaking their thoughts candidly on a daily basis—which I saw as a primary reason for getting rid of reviews.

You see, I believed the mainstream culture had the thinking behind performance reviews 100 percent inside out.[4] It had people believing that reviews were necessary in order for employees to receive performance feedback and to learn. I saw them differently. Reviews intimidated employees. They prevented employees from telling managers about the problems their "good management behavior" created for them. Get rid of reviews, modify the structure, and then managers will finally have access to the type of feedback they can learn from—rather than the other way around.

> One of the leaders "ran the initiative by 'Bill,'" the CEO of the company, and assured "the leadership group" that Bill was "on board" with getting rid of reviews.
>
> Eventually it was time to get HR operatives involved. The company's personnel-and-retention procedures and training policies needed revising to reflect what the compensation professionals had worked out. The leaders also wanted HR operatives to work up an implementation plan, alpha and beta test it, and make revisions to avoid glitches discovered in these test runs. HR operatives were also needed to frame internal announcements and manage the logistics for geographically separate, departmentally appropriate roll-outs. The leaders asked me to advise these HR people as well.

I thought it important that roll-outs include a segment that helps people, managers in particular, *unlock from the illogic* that was used for so many years in justifying reviews, corresponding to the recommendations I made in chapter 7. Debunking would also help managers to see there would be no turning back.

Most managers are accustomed to a self-directed focus and, probably more than they're consciously aware, rely on direct reports knowing they are being scored. I anticipated that relinquishing this source of dominance would arouse resistances (mental speedbumps) that would need engaging. With reviews no longer in the picture, managers also needed supports for transitioning to relationships that would no longer tolerate the control and intimidating tactics that, formerly, they could get away with. For supports I suggested manager-buddy system pairings and same-level-manager support groups.

The leaders had the big picture. They understood that while the initiative was about getting rid of reviews, the real issue was removing barriers to employees speaking candidly. They saw employee voice as a boost to managers recognizing their "good management" behavior faults, and evolving a more other-directed mentality. Leaders also saw getting rid of reviews as a lessening of manager-caused employee alienation.

The HR people never seemed to get this reasoning. Their focus was on performing the specific tasks assigned them with excellence.

As is often the case with large company initiatives, there were many stops and restarts due to leadership assignments changing, and exigencies of the day taking precedence. There was also a year-long *interruption* when the initiative was superseded by the roll-out of a CEO-led Core Values and Company Mission Statement to be engaged by all employees worldwide. This initiative was to be reified in quarterly "Performance and Development" discussions where each direct report answered three open-ended questions, with their manager commenting on what they said:

1. *What have you accomplished and contributed to the company?*
2. *How has your work exemplified the company's mission and core values?*
3. *Beyond your designated role, what's been your impact on other people and their success?*

To my way of thinking, the core values initiative was anything but an interruption; it was an enhancement to the initiative on which I was assisting. With a couple of procedural adjustments, the two initiatives knitted together extremely well. That's because the core values initiative provided managers the two types of acknowledgement and credit people need when assuming an other-directed focus. They got credit for their own accomplishments and they got credit for helping others accomplish.

With new levels of employee candor forthcoming, and with managers facing upcoming opportunities to hear what their reports had formerly withheld, I saw the opportunity to promote everyone's learning by adding a fourth question for both managers and reports to answer.

4. *What have you learned about how you have been managing (or operating) that causes you to behave differently now?*

Answering this question would allow managers to earn credit for self-critiquing and having their self-improvement efforts noted and gains recognized. It addressed a primary reason for getting rid of reviews.

The performance and development discussions were formatted to be one-sided and hierarchical. It had direct reports accounting, and managers commenting—as is the status quo practice in boss-dominant, hierarchical relationships. For managers to learn, that format needed revising.

Personally, I've never been concerned about employees receiving enough feedback, and using what they thought accurate to improve as they were able. But consistent with the accounts I've been reporting in this book, there are plenty of reasons for worrying about managers having sufficient incentive to self-question, and to contemplate what's dysfunctional in their relationships with employees. Absent performance reviews, direct reports would have fewer reasons to hold back.

Instead of just one person taking stock of the other's performance, I suggested both manager and direct report should self-critique and partner in a "joint learning and improvement discussion." I recommended they flip a coin to decide who would go first. That person then relates what he or she has accomplished, contributed to others, and personally learned about better ways of managing or operating, and now is looking to do better. The second person listens, makes notes, and waits their turn to likewise self-report.

Following initial presentations, I recommended manager and direct report hold an interactive exchange. This could even include responding to what the other person stated based on their own experiences. With performance reviews gone,[5] each could benefit from some no-bad-consequences candid feedback and critique. And, at least hypothetically, as long as discussants each stick to the first-person pronoun, neither should have much to lose by being wrong, or possibly recanting and revising. Each would merely be reporting their thinking in the moment, and referencing their experience and how they interpreted it. There would be little need to pretend agreement; if they agree, they really agree. And, going forward, they would have many opportunities to support and help one another self-improve.

What's more, each person has several self-assessment and improvement discussions. The boss has like discussions with his or her manager and other direct reports; the subordinate with his or her direct reports. That's for starters. Over time it all gets modified as personal aspirations, chemistry, and work situations dictate. With performance reviews gone, there's no gun-to-the-head false agreements. What's heard is dismissible or useable, as each person decides for themselves.

Now let me ask you, absent the physical presence of a committed leader, what reaction do you think I received from HR professionals for advocating the fourth question and an adjusted format? I'll give you a hint. It wasn't a "yes" and it wasn't a "no." Good, you guessed it. I got the ol' noncommittal, "We'll take it under advisement." No mystery in my mind as to what that meant.

In comparison, every top-level manager and leader in the company was actively involved in rolling out the CEO-led core values initiative, and there was no one quibbling about the use of those three questions, the one-side-accountable format, and a set date for each quarter's discussion.

It was time for me to alert initiative leaders that the process was faltering and in need of reinvigoration. Without their active involvement I feared the "getting rid of reviews" initiative wouldn't realize its mentality-evolving goal. Performance reviews would be removed, but the main benefits would remain unrealized.

The Buck Stops at the Top

It's not where I started out, and it's not what I idealize, but it's a lesson that's been verified for me time and time again. The management mentality that's prevalent in a company is the responsibility of the company's CEO. Yes, the culture at large can be fairly blamed for a good deal of bad management, but it's the CEO's responsibility to take stock of the prevailing management mentality and to either own it or work to get it upgraded. It's a responsibility that needs to be taken seriously, and requires vigilant monitoring. Managerial behavior affects people's lives and workplace effectiveness far too much to receive casual treatment. That's why I went ballistic in the "CEO thank-you note incident" I related in chapter 6. No company can afford that type of out-of-touch obliviousness for long.

The CEO doesn't have to come up with a coherent plan on his or her own, and other top-level leaders can be assigned to lead an initiative. However, the CEO needs to make sure that managers clearly know what's expected of them, and have processes in place that can move managers closer to the mentality the leader wants acquired. In the aforementioned case, quarterly performance and development discussions are such a process. But if the process doesn't have the CEO's wholehearted backing, it's unlikely any substantial change will occur, no matter who serves as CEO-designated leader.

Stipulating Behavior Accomplishes Little

It's not unusual for leaders to have strong opinions about which attributes, behaviors, and interpersonal styles are the best ones for managers to assume. What most leaders realize, but seldom mention, is that no single attribute, in and of itself, is ever sufficient. Every positive has a downside, and what's desirable in one situation can be counterproductive in another. Metaphorically speaking, a kick in the butt never makes anyone's list of desirables, but situations arise where a well-timed "kick" serves as a tough love–administered wake-up call received.

On the other hand, "intelligence" is always considered a big positive. Yet we're all familiar with the expression, "That person is too smart for their own good." Of course, when such a statement is made, there's usually a bit of "misspeak" involved. The person voicing that opinion is actually referring to *their* "own good." Whatever the list of positive behaviors or attributes mentioned, the criteria used mirror the logic voiced by Supreme Court justice Potter Stewart when ruling on what constitutes pornography. Most people believe they know enough about good management "to know it when they see it" taking place.

I see insisting on specific behaviors as a mistake. Doing so allows people to change behavior without changing underlying sentiments and attitude. It's analogous to how a person conforming to the letter of a law can ignore the purpose the law was conceived to serve. For example, a colleague showed me her list of twenty companies whose management alleges they've abolished performance reviews. But each of the companies that I personally knew about still had pay, bonus, and job assignment connected to a managers' discretionary ratings of employees. So tell me, what did these companies achieve in the way of more candid manager/direct report conversations? I bet little changed in the deferential treatment and absence of candor their managers receive.

I much prefer managers to have experiences that provoke self-reflection and self-questioning than to see them enacting leader-prescribed behaviors. I find it far more effective when leaders provide processes that allow managers, on their own, to experience the benefits of mind-sets conducive to the mentality the leader wants company employees to receive. Since each manager has different skills, attributes, personal proclivities, and blind spots to overcome, it makes sense to leave it to them to figure out how to behave.

Mind-Sets That Support an Other-Directed Management Mentality

I have a starter list of five mind-set destinations that support other-directedness in management. In considering them, keep in mind that I'm merely talking about one dimension of a manager's job—staging for others to accomplish and succeed. For the foreseeable future, managers who neglect their own accomplishing, or their accountability for work-unit results, will have good reason to feel insecure.

Think of the mind-sets I list as destinations that managers seeking to acquire a more other-directed focus will benefit from visiting and exploring. Think of the processes that leaders provide—and I will mention several of them shortly—as vehicles for traveling to, and sojourning in, those mind-set destinations. Add in recognition that, by nature, people feel compelled to take distinctly different routes. Applying this model, leaders stipulate destinations (mind-sets), provide vehicles (processes), offer route guidance, inquire when they fear the tenability of the route they see a manager taking, and insist on rescuing individuals who seem lost.

When it comes to mind-sets, I prefer leaders to think in degrees, modicums, and enhancements. I don't like people thinking about mind-sets as absolutes. If you talk absolutes, such as the numbers used in performance reviews, there's a good chance of a discussion deteriorating to "What do I need to do to get from a 4.7 to a 5.0?" Such conversations quickly become slippery slopes to the ridiculous. Not only do they waste time, they consume precious goodwill.

With all of that in mind, here are five mind-set destinations:

1. Managers need to *feel secure.*

Feeling secure is the bedrock mind-set in Maslow's hierarchy of needs.[6] Managers need a sense of well-being—psychological safety and job security—to release from self-concerns so they can focus on the concerns of people they're supposed to assist.

I've already discussed many of the perils managers face that are caused by work-culture expectations—the pretense needed for maintaining image, the vulnerability incurred in doing so, and the feelings of insecurity that follow. I've also described the importance amassing a record of tangible accomplishments serves in allowing managers to feel secure— safeguarding feelings of vulnerability and documenting their worth. Herein lies the crux of the problem befalling managers. Other-directed efforts don't yield tangible accomplishments. They don't make managers feel more secure. In fact, it's the opposite. There's little immediate output; the relationship-building transaction costs are high; and what's documentable is usually hearsay, fleeting, and intangible.

People feel secure when they think they're performing high-quality work, and believe key others see them as essential contributors. Two sources of affirmation are involved. The first is self-valuing of the work performed. The second is having key others—company leaders and a person's boss—value the output, and whether the performer sees these people as having a valid basis for what they positively conclude.

Leaders wanting more other-directedness need processes in place that acknowledge the value of efforts and contributions made. That's what the four questions in the case study were aimed at establishing. The first three—"What have you accomplished?"; "How have you supported company values?"; and "What have you helped others to accomplish?"—acknowledge other-directedness delivered. The fourth question—"What have you learned?"—credits managers for acquiring the personal resourcefulness that makes yet higher-quality contributions possible. It's all process. If managers weren't provided this process, what evidence would they have that the time consumed assisting others was productively spent?

2. Managers should make *authenticity and integrity* a goal in every exchange.

The easiest and most natural way of promoting a mind-set of *authenticity and integrity* is by leaders walking the talk, being their natural, open-spirit, flawed, and highest integrity, authentically expressive selves. Notice I didn't include adjectives like *self-centered, self-indulgent,* or *narcissistic.* That stuff should be left on the golf course. At work people look to leaders as exemplars, and need their other-directed focus and support to work their best.

For managers to drop their guards and be their authentic selves, they need to believe that what's revealed won't be used to diminish them. It's not that managers should expect others, especially leaders, to overlook their faults, miscues, and imperfections, it's that they need to believe that owing up won't disqualify them, or cast aspersions on the value of what they contribute and competently perform.

In chapter 7, I spoke at length about the integrity demonstrated when leaders admit short-sightedness, and own up to mistaken reasoning. For leaders who thrive on hierarchy,

I recognize this can be asking a lot. Everyone acts defensively when facing the consequences of an error. Why not merely correct and move ahead? Because admitting error, and repairing what was damaged, communicates far more than any words one can speak. I'm talking about two-sided, leaders-included, lessons-learned accountability. Processes like these make authenticity and integrity possible.

Far and away the most impactful way I know for leaders to support an authenticity and integrity mind-set is by insisting people use the first-person pronoun. Teaching I-Speak to students, and advocating its use with clients, I've heard many accounts of transformed relationships. Saying something as pedestrian as, "Let me tell you how I see it . . ." immediately does away with false objectivity. *Speaking in the first person, an individual is never wrong.* Unless too intimidated, the other person is free to say, "I see it differently." If that person doesn't, it's a goodwill courtesy to inquire, "How do you see it?" I-Speak allows a manager to be high-integrity and authentic, even under the most challenging conditions.

3. Managers should be encouraged to take a *systems view* of how their actions impact others, and, more generally, organization-wide teamwork.

In chapter 3, I spoke skeptically about the "senior leadership team" and the reluctance I've seen top-tier managers have to assuming a company well-being mind-set. In chapter 5, I spoke about managers' fear of cohorts and the self-protective routines used to keep cohorts at bay. Now I want to acknowledge the beneficial results possible when managers see one another looking out for their interests, and feeling sufficiently secure to assume a "one for all and all for one" systems-view mind-set. That's the paramount tool any CEO needs to take a company forward.

It's time to accept that self-interests are inextricably intertwined in all work agendas, and it's across-the-board ineffective that most people find it necessary to pretend otherwise. It's a fact that needs acknowledgement and to be made an organization-wide "discussable." When someone doesn't understand where another person is coming from, they should feel free to inquire. It provides agenda-seekers cause for self-discipline, and it provides agenda-questioners an opportunity to correct what they misinterpret. Keep in mind the presence of self-interests does not equate to unrelenting selfishness or uncompromising competitiveness. Couple this fact with acceptance of another: an organization is a system in which any work unit–initiated activity is likely to impact other work units and their operatives.

A systems-view mind-set obligates managers to notify affected parties of their agendas and activities, and inquire into anticipated ramifications. It provides the motivation for envisaging ripple effects, and negotiating modifications prior to problems being unleashed. And when the unanticipated occurs, this mind-set obligates problem-initiators to make themselves part of the solution. Likewise, when managers see people in other jurisdictions taking action that impacts their work units, the systems-view mind-set provides the rationale for making their agendas known.

The systems-view mind-set obligates managers to align all agendas pursued with company-first outcomes. Of course, this is what everyone pretends, but it's different when personal agendas are explicitly known. Other-directed thoughtfulness should extend to the needs of every part of the organization. Hearing about problems faced by others should evoke empathy, a willingness to lend a hand or to contribute an idea, and receptivity to those who offer. Interconnectedness should be sought when silos are noticed and communication problems in other areas become everyone's pressing concern.

Of course, the more information bearing on marketplace conditions and strategic issues facing the company that managers have, the better job of teaming up and coordinating they can perform. As much as any other-directed preparatory mind-set, this one benefits from leaders sharing as much strategic information as prudently possible.

4. Managers should be *self-managing* and *in charge* of their own development.

Here's a mind-set that saves enormous time and prevents needless upset. Assign managers to manage themselves, including taking charge of their own development. Then, as rigorously as possible, hold them self-accountable for performing these functions. By self-accountable, I mean, "Leader, resist seizing the authority." Inquire when you have doubts. Keep current by asking managers what they're doing. Tell them your worries. But no heavy-handed stipulating that undermines the authority you've delegated. If it becomes necessary, throw out the baby (manager), not the bathwater (process). You'll need that process for dealings with other managers. Of course, I'm talking destinations and vehicles.

Situation permitting, I find the criterion *no surprises* without equal in supporting managers' adoption of a *self-managing* mind-set. It's relatively straight-forward to communicate, and easy to monitor. Immediately it makes the manager the responsible party for getting positive results. If the manager needs information, additional resources, or even a sounding-board adviser, it's that manager's responsibility to communicate what's needed and get it accomplished. If a manager tells their boss something is going to happen, that boss should assume it will until an instant after the manager believes differently. At that point, everyone who needs to know what's tenuous, or needed for a repair, should receive a heads-up notice. If that doesn't happen, talk about the missing notification, not the repair. Support the process.

Whatever the end result, relevant people should see it coming. If there's a surprise, the manager stands lessons-learned accountable to themselves. In the early 1900s, Frederick Taylor coined the term "management by exception," and wrote about the efficiencies of low-keying management when operations are running smoothly.[7] What I'm describing entails more communication than what Taylor advocated, yet it captures the efficiency of doing away with needless oversight.

The self-managing mind-set puts managers *in charge of their own development*, self-assessing and responsible for learning what's needed to personally progress. If a manager wants a leader's opinion, or anyone else's, it's their responsibility to access it. And if it was me that a manager consulted, I already know what my response would be. It's the way I always respond. I ask the "How do you see it?" question. People live complicated lives, and even when I think I know enough about the next improvement a person needs to make, it's unlikely I'd know that individual's priorities and capacity for learning about it.

5. Managers should make *interpersonal competence* and *personably rewarding relationships* a priority.

Much of the bad behavior I've been describing results from managers' insensitivity to direct reports, self-protective defensiveness with cohorts, and generally treating of people as a means to an end—turning on social niceties as their personal agendas require. Too many friendships are relationships of convenience where *friends* aren't actually friends. Try this question: Who in the company treats HR people as "friends"? Answer: "Everybody." Question: When those HR people are not in the room, how many *friends* do they have? Answer: *Not nearly as many.* Get my drift?

Managers may refer to their reports as *teammates* and *partners*, refer to cohorts as *colleagues*, and call everyone in the company their *friend*, but don't fall for the rhetoric. Most people get dealt with instrumentally, as collaborators and allies of convenience, not spoken to authentically or treated as "I've got your back" friends. I'm not talking about all managers, or many managers every time out. But I am talking about enough most of the time, and I have many reasons for believing this.

Too seldom do managers value the people with whom they work for the affiliation, friendship, "we're in it together" learning, and feelings of intimacy afforded from just associating with good people. Few give much thought to accessing human-richness qualities. When I ask in the continuing education classroom, I find most managers inclined to slough off what I'm intimating on the grounds that their days are full and they lack time for anything more. And many don't seem to have any idea of what they might gain until I give them a questionnaire[8] and exercise for experiencing the essence of another person, as I do with scores of people annually. Many are amazed by the humanity they experience in a mere hour-long conversation with others. And they are equally amazed by the humanity it draws out in *themselves* as they learn to connect with someone on a more intimate level.

How to account for managers not realizing the preciousness of the humanity around them? Is it fear of exposure of the pretentious and self-interested actions one takes that, in a straight-talking relationship, would immediately be made apparent? Is it for lack of knowing how to approach people, and the possibility of suffering a rejection? Perhaps it's out of anticipation of eventual loss when they, or someone with whom they've bonded, moves on. Perhaps it's for lack of family role models and not having experienced the type of intimacy to which I've been alluding.

Whatever the reasons, I find most of the pretentious, manipulative, and instrumental relationships taking place at work to be missed opportunities. Lack of an other-directed focus becomes a self-fulfilling prophesy. Managers don't look for more; they don't receive it; they don't know what's there; and they don't even realize they're missing out. That's why this mind-set is needed.

Conclusion

I know of no sure-fire way of getting leaders to commit the thoughtfulness, energy, and company resources required for evolving the managerial mentality in their company. Clearly they have the means. Where do they get the will to use it?

Managers entrapped, entangled in cultural pretense, fearful of being exposed and criticized; operatives entrapped, at their peril to authentically express their thoughts and feelings. What can an individual do?

I believe there are actions any concerned party can take in prodding leaders to take ownership of the management mentality that prevails in their company, and to take steps in making it what they want. That's what I'll be describing next.

Notes

1. Jack Welch did it with a three-week management school at GE; Neil McElroy did it installing a brand-manager mentality at Procter & Gamble; Mark Shahriary did it leading a three-company consortium to put an Internet in the sky that was put on hold when the tech bubble burst in 2000.
2. L.V. Gerstner, *Who Says Elephants Can't Dance?* (New York: Harper, 2002).
3. A.J. Dunlap, *Mean Business* (New York: Random House, 1996).
4. S.A. Culbert and L. Rout, *Get Rid of the Performance Review! How Companies Can Stop the Intimidating, Start Managing, and Focus on What Really Matters* (New York: Business Plus, 2010).
5. Recall, interlocking systems had been removed.
6. A.H. Maslow, *Motivation and Personality* (New York: Harper, 1954).
7. F.W. Taylor, *The Principles of Scientific Management* (Mineola, NY: Dover Publications, 1998).
8. See Appendix A in S.A. Culbert, *Beyond Bullsh*t: Straight-Talk at Work* (Palo Alto, CA: Stanford University Press, 2008).

9

CONSCIOUSNESS-RAISING TO PROMOTE OTHER-DIRECTEDNESS IN MANAGEMENT

A trap is a trap only for a creature which cannot solve the problems that it sets. Man-traps are dangerous only in relation to the limitations on what men can see and value and do. The nature of the trap is a function of the nature of the trapped. To describe either is to imply the other.

Geoffrey Vickers[1]

I see managers ensnared in a work-culture-set trap. Having internalized what the culture falsely stipulates, lacking incentives to reason otherwise, managers are unaware of the problems their culture-stipulated "good management behavior" creates.

It's not their intent to act badly. Pretense prevents them from connecting the dots. To be intentional, managers would have to connect what they don't see themselves doing to effectiveness problems their reports won't tell them they are having.

In their minds they're practicing good management. That's why I've been calling their dereliction and bad behavior *"inadvertent,"* caused by "limitations on what [they] can see and value and do." I like the way Vickers depicts it: "The nature of the trap is a function of the nature of the trapped. To describe either is to imply the other."

The culture has managers pretending to be objective, ever-collaborative, company-first thinkers and action-takers. Deep down, managers know they're anything but that. But owning up is self-incriminating. Intimidated, insecure, and pretentiously thinking they should be what they are not, most managers lack the means to be authentically expressive. Once people interacting with them spot their duplicity, there's no way to earn their trust.

I find managers standing too close to the screen to take in what they effect. They need to step back and view the entire picture to realize they haven't been doing nearly as well as they've been telling themselves. Their direct reports are on to their duplicitous ways—and taking the dereliction quite personally.

Reports shouldn't take it personally. In most instances, it's the system staging the dramas and writing the scripts managers enact. What's transpiring is the result of how managers feel forced to act. But employees do take it personally. What's transpiring affects their lives and their dreams. It's natural to resent the manager whose inaction deprives them of so much of what they want and need.

Operatives Are Trapped

Ensnared in vulnerability, operatives are also trapped. They sign on thinking they're going to work for a company. They come with ideas of contributing, and expectations of getting ahead for doing so. Eventually they figure out their employer is not the entity writing the checks: it's a self-focused manager. Their job is accomplishing what this manager self-interestedly alleges the company needs, and in the way that person wants it performed.

At some point operatives try to discuss the negatives, but nothing of substance gets altered. Gradually, operatives lose hope that their problems will ever count. Knuckling under to authority, they mute their voice.

Lacking power, operatives become preoccupied with concern for how they are being viewed. Viewed by the company? No. By the manager to whom they report. Everything they produce, and every interaction, seems to bear on future prospects. It all seems to hinge on one individual's portrayal of the work they produce, and too often that seems to depend on whether that individual likes them.

By this time, most operatives realize they're on their own, and feeling vulnerable because of this. They're imperfect, lack voice, in need of guidance, coaching, and support, and hungry for a sign of appreciation for what they've been knocking themselves out to produce. Most of all, they need what the system seldom provides: a manager with an other-directed focus helping them get ahead. That's what they took the job expecting. The advertisement attracting them to apply didn't include "self-preoccupied manager" on its list of benefits.

Getting an Other-Directed Focus Is Chancy

The point has been made: without company leaders involved, people aren't going to receive the other-directed, good management behavior they need. Yes, some will get it, and some will get along much better than others without it. And while everyone would be better off receiving more, the majority won't get much.

While most leaders acknowledge the importance of what I've labeled an "other-directed managerial focus," few leaders find the benefits sufficiently attractive to commit to a process for evolving it. To commit, a leader would have to believe the time and energy required would net big bottom-line payoffs. Few leaders hold such a view. For one thing, where would they acquire it? Certainly not in school. I don't know a single finance professor who stresses anything like the bottom-line impact of other-directed, good management behavior.

How about personal values as the driver? Would work-life enrichment for everyone in the company be sufficient motivation for leaders to devote themselves to the process? Personally, I can't imagine many going for this, particularly with the uncertainties involved. But we don't really know, so let's leave this an open question. In any event, I find it unfortunate that having someone at the top leading a change-management initiative is far and away the best course to take in getting managers to evolve. Given the stakes, I don't like the odds.

Stepping back, I see an unfortunate mismatch. Top-level leaders have the means, but most won't see sufficient gains to justify the effort required. The economy has turned around, their companies are profitable, and people burdened by bad management behavior are neither loudly complaining nor defecting in numbers that cause them much angst. And what about the people who know what they have to gain? The people who believe everyone's effectiveness and well-being would be greatly enhanced, with big bottom-line payouts following. Well, they lack the means. What can people do besides look out for themselves and grumble?

What You Can Do

I wrote this book thinking that enhanced awareness of the cultural forces perverting good management behavior, and the false premises on which those forces are based, would prove useful in helping people cope with what is not in their power to change. I also saw a good amount of self-enabling that people at any level of hierarchy can perform—and at least two very constructive purposes served by their doing so: first, for-ease-of-mind comfort and enhanced self-effectiveness; second, for communicating their company experience in sufficiently compelling terms to incentivize leaders to use their *means*. Along these lines, I have two approaches to suggest.[2]

Each approach begins with self-reflection on the discordant feelings provoked by a specific managerial action. The first entails raising one's awareness of the specific causes of those feelings—messages received, sensitivities evoked, symbolism involved, mentalities inferred, et cetera—for purposes of catharsis, and enhanced personal functioning going forward. The second approach entails exchanging insights with *friendly* cohorts for purposes of heightened awareness, bonding, and, eventually, to spur leaders into thinking about the management mentality in their company with the idea of getting involved. The task is not formulating the ultimate argument that no leader can resist. It's unlikely any mortal could accomplish that. The task is to participate in a process that makes management actions discussable, and creates enough buzz that top-level leaders take notice and eventually feel the need to get out in front leading a mentality-evolving effort.

Approach No. 1: Consciousness-Raising for Enhanced Awareness Going Forward

Approach #1 takes the discordant feelings as prima facie evidence of a person's alienation. Through the use of inductive reasoning, the individual seeks to identify what was communicated by the specific action that evoked those feelings, and, perhaps, more generally communicated by the management mentality represented by that action. Minimally, the managerial action alienated the person experiencing discordance; possibly that action signifies a mentality that would alienate a preponderance of like-stationed individuals; and maybe what's communicated by this specific action is also communicated in other similar in-character managerial actions system wide. This approach seeks to identify what is being communicated and the extent of the impact it has.

Whatever the specifics, consider two types of provocation. In type A, management expects something—an action, attitude, thought process, or identity—that the individual finds inconsistent with his or her inner nature, temperament, and/or goals and self-interested pursuits. Alternatively, in type B, management disapproves of and/or actively censures a way of being, or performing work, that seems self-appropriate and congruent with one's inner nature. An example of the former is found in the story about the manager whose home life was being eaten away by what he thought it took to prove himself worthy at work (described in chapter 1). An example of the latter is the story about the applicant who received the dressing down that shook his confidence for ten years and running (also in chapter 1). It's a shame neither of these men were able to grasp the impersonality of the events causing them so much alienation, or to learn how experiencing events like these is part and parcel of their indoctrination in a management mentality that unleashes situations like the ones that upset them.

Now decide: A or B? This is the first step in clarifying what's askew in the management mentality that negatively impacts on your well-being.

Then reflect: Is this a message you're likely to encounter in the actions of other managers, or is it unique to your interaction with the manager involved in this specific situation? If it's this manager and not others, it could be due to differences in temperament, bias, chemistry—there could be any number of causes. That should be relatively easy to determine. Once determined, you can decide what action, if any, to take with respect to this specific occurrence. It could be setting someone straight on a misperception of you; it could be apologizing for overreacting to a sensitivity created by interacting with someone in your past (personal baggage).

Most often, what's bothersome is widespread in the prevailing managerial mentality and causes alienation in other like-situated people. It could be any type of alienation: feelings caused by having one's opinion dismissed, lack of fair

play, not being consulted, something prejudicial or discrimi-
natory, being lumped in a category, or just about any managerial action that rubs you the wrong way. Next, consider what
about the way managers think puts you, this time, and others at other times, on the defensive. See how precise you can
be in naming the message implied by the specific action that
bothered you.

The second part of this consciousness-raising approach
utilizes inductive reasoning to further analyze what you've
uncovered. It's analogous to examining fossil DNA scrapings
for the purpose of reconstructing the dinosaur from which
they came. One reflects, "What does this incoherent event
reveal about the prevailing management mentality in the
company?"

Inductively, one performs what I term "Why, This, Now"
investigative work.[3] What's just been identified serves as the
"clue"; now the task is to learn about the system that produced
it. One inquires, *"Why* is *this* message being sent out *now*?"—
with *now* being the situation or circumstance that prompted
it. See how many specifics you can reasonably induce.
Reflect: What purpose was this discordance-arousing message intended to serve? Who benefits, and how? What forces
bear on the person initiating it? What assumptions are being
made about you and your role, and which of them are inappropriate? Who and what are allowing what's wrongly assumed
to endure and continue managerially unnoticed? If messages
like this weren't being sent, what would be missing in the way
managers operate here, and how would that gap be filled? If
some modifications were made to correct it, what fears might
be evoked, and from whom? Ask any question that seems relevant to teasing out implications from what you just put under
the microscope.

Do you need examples? Think about the discordant feelings evoked by managerial actions we've already discussed.
Discordant feelings from operatives having to work off-
the-clock so their manager can bring a project in on budget

(chapter 1); from being in a meeting where the CEO asks someone to mislead the client because the company needs the additional income (chapter 2); from watching a manager defer on
training replacements for retiring engineers in order to ensure
bonus-deserving numbers (chapter 2); and from observing
top-level managers engage in self-protective routines like the
ones mentioned in chapter 5. And I haven't even touched on
all the waste-of-time meetings or the time-consuming reading
of emails sent by individuals fearful of offending by putting
people in an information loop that holds little value for them.
Keep in mind I'm talking about other people's situations. Try
this approach on a gut-gnawing situation in your work life
today. You'll be amazed. It's like going out fishing and having
the fish jump into your boat.

Approach No. 2: Consciousness-Raising for Company Gain

What if people experiencing self-focused management stood
their ground and spoke forthrightly about aspects of the managerial mentality that negatively impact their effectiveness—
and intrude on their lives outside of work? What if, when the
emperor appeared with no clothes, someone had the gump-
tion to blurt out, "I beg your pardon, Your Majesty, your shirt
needs tucking in the back."

Company leaders need to know what people think, whatever it is, and people need to express it—if only to provide
the leader an opportunity to set them straight and get them
back on course. Most of all, leaders need people to hold their
ground when they push back. They almost always push back.
Personally, I believe providing one's differing beliefs to people
with power is a profound act of loyalty that shouldn't come at
personal risk. But it frequently does, and people feeling they
lost out by doing so often resolve, "Never again!"

Leaders need to hear about management problems often
enough to realize that the company's management mentality
is an issue that's not going away. The more accounts they hear,

the greater likelihood they'll get the point. They know that leaving obvious flaws unaddressed threatens their credibility. They also realize that single-point solutions seldom get the underlying issue resolved. Their need to do what's right, combined with concern for maintaining a positive image, will be enough to motivate most. Now, how do we get people to reveal their bad management experiences without jeopardizing their relationships with the managers perpetrating them?

Two tasks are involved. First you must frame a message sufficiently compelling that most people hearing it, leaders in particular, feel a need to engage it as serious. The second is finding the means to not back down when a leader pushes back. The latter is a tall order for people who fear being seen insubordinate, or labeled "negative."

Formulating a Compelling Message

Approach No. 1 allows you to identify others whose effectiveness you believe is similarly hampered by the mentality issue troubling you. Of course, each individual possesses unique skills, background sensitivities, et cetera, so expect the negative impact it holds for another person, and the feelings of alienation provoked, to inevitably be somewhat different than they are for you. Contrasting experiences, sharing insights, and dialoging should deepen your understanding. It almost always will sharpen your thinking and improve your articulation of the issues commanding your attention. It's also an opportunity to dry-run how you'll want to portray your thoughts when an opportunity occurs to describe them to a leader.

The very good news is that no one has sole responsibility for advancing any viewpoint, nor does it depend only on one person's awareness. Everyone in a company has a stake in the management mentality evolving, even managers whose current behavior is a source of discordance. Others also read management books, and ardently reflect on management events.

It takes time for any new way of looking at managerial behavior to take root. Most people feel the need to sort things out for themselves. Some will *rerun their tapes* of past events to see what their new awareness reveals, and whether their reactions now make more sense. Many will be wanting to see if and how their new awareness makes ensuing events more understandable.

One last bit of practical advice: I urge caution in choosing "friends" for sharing. Until the management mentality in a company evolves, there will be insecure-feeling people who, when representing someone's words and sentiments to third parties, will do so in a way that reflects their in-the-moment competitive motives more than the character and intent of the person who told them. It's going to happen, and you're not going to be present to correct them. When you get wind of it, set the record straight as best you can without criticizing the person misrepresenting you. Even when angry, do your best to speak respectfully about everyone, not just those in the room.

Standing Your Ground

I've already provided the best means I know for an individual to stand their ground and get their views across: I-Speak. Using I-Speak allows a person to matter-of-factly tell anyone their views and reactions, and the meaning they extract from what they see transpiring, without appearing disrespectful.

There are a few caveats here that I believe a person prudently should keep in mind. Keep your comments to issues, not people. Remember that the problems you're having stem from the prevailing mentality, and this time it just happens to be imperfect person X reifying it; next time it'll be imperfect person Y; and you could be imperfect person Z. In other words, speak about the *virus*, don't assail the virus carrier. If there's bad behavior or unfairness, keep your comments to the system that provokes it and tolerates it. People will get defensive; you can't prevent that. But there's no need to pin the problem on an individual. Besides, once your ideas about the *virus*, sink in, you'll want everyone, including today's virus carriers, helping to eradicate it.

People have many options for sharing their insights, and many serendipitous opportunities to speak them. Whatever you decide, be sure to check whether the individual you're addressing is in a listening mood. That person won't be if they are preoccupied with another agenda, or hold strong views they feel compelled to defend. Since you already know what you want to say, why not let the other person speak first. Start by asking how he or she sees the issue. Then speak in terms that correspond to the words and issues the person just expressed. If you think you already know, I recommend inquiring anyway. You might begin with, "Here's how I understand your views; set me straight on what I have incorrect." Afterwards, it's enough to say, "I see it differently, and I'd like to tell you why." No need to get argumentative; use a friendly tone that invites the other person's interest.

If, after you've presented your views, that person decides to set you straight, it's best to listen without interrupting. If you disagree and don't think you can make progress pressing your views, there's no need to counter. Your silence lets them know they didn't prevail. Take your best shot and leave it at that. You've shared your reality, and the other person now knows what you believe. People remember differences in opinion and tensions much longer than they remember agreement. That's an established fact.[4]

Leaders and Managers Can Do More

I find managers and leaders self-deluding when they think they and their companies have access to most of the critical issues weighing on people's minds. Most will say they want to hear more, and I believe them. But how can they reasonably believe they know what concerns individual employees given the systems they have in place?

I'm always looking for ways to remove the system roadblocks to leaders and managers hearing the real concerns on people's minds. I've been mentioning them throughout this book. Get hierarchy out of relationships, and insist on no surprises; get rid of performance reviews, and remove the intimidation; stop the punishing, and implement lessons-learned accountability; reward other-directed management behavior; ask managers what they learned, and, then, what blocked them from knowing it sooner; when making an improvement, acknowledge the faulty logic formerly used; promote and provide supports for straight-talk relationships; maximize transparency; make it possible for people to be up-front with their agendas; conduct political vying in the daylight; make the system fair, irrespective of personality—I can go on mentioning what systemically impairs employees sharing perspectives and facts their leaders and managers should know.

Without knowing what others truly think, managers and leaders can't do what's right for themselves, let alone for the people they rely on for getting company work accomplished. And, as I've already mentioned, the work culture at large is full of obstacles that prevent leaders from finding out. The person who can help the most is that leader, once they figure out how important it is to know. Recall that my reason for getting rid of performance reviews wasn't just to save time and prevent resentment. It was to enable managers to hear what others truly think and to learn lessons needed for bettering themselves as managers. Why am I optimistic that company leaders will realize this and eventually reverse course? Because once they open their eyes, their good intentions will push most of them to do what's right. When not on the defense, goodwilled people look for opportunities to self-improve and do good turns for others. That's a wonderful part of human nature. Lots of people come with this type of character and integrity.

Now let me put it to them directly. Ms. Leader, Mr. Manager, if you really want to know what's going on, make it possible for people to tell you. You don't have to have a fix. You just have to do your best and show appreciation when people are forthright in telling you. Respect message carriers; don't get stuck only thinking about what they stand to gain. Be open about your limitations. The big opportunity is allowing messages to get in. You're ahead just by knowing what's going on in the lives and thinking of people. Afterwards, you'll have plenty of time to figure out the response you want to make.

When listening, try to dig down from specifics to figure out what's going on in the system that produces symptoms like the ones people are telling you about now. That's where the opportunities lie. Think about the CEO of Volkswagen,[5] who didn't know his company's engineering managers were outsmarting US government regulators. He alleges no one inside the company told him, and that he found out the same way the rest of us did, watching the news. While I didn't believe that, I did believe him when he said he wished he had known it in time to stop it. Why didn't he know? Why did it happen? Probably because he set internal goals that people couldn't meet without cheating, and they didn't feel free to push back and tell him that.

I've observed many companies try processes aimed at ensuring leaders and managers learn what lower-down managers and employees think. Noteworthy for me is what the Home Depot founders created by assigning board members a quarterly quota of store aisles to walk—holding confidential discussions with employees encouraged to tell them everything that mattered. Formulating what they learned as system issues, board members held top-level managers responsible for getting the systems that created the problems they heard about appropriately revised and fixed. This intelligence-seeking paid off when the corporation was hit with a women's equity, class-action law suit.[6] No one was surprised, and management was ahead of the game, having documented several ameliorating actions taken.

I saw a good system for sensing what was on people's minds used by Procter & Gamble engineering managers in the 1970s.

It's one I've helped managers in other companies adapt and implement. Engineers wrote bimonthly white papers on topics pertinent to productivity and quality of work life. Institutional learning was promoted by each manager being asked to write reports detailing what they were personally contemplating based on reading, and sometimes discussing, the concerns and effectiveness issues on the minds of their reports. In turn, these papers were forwarded up the chain for total management awareness and possible discussion.

Last, I'd like to mention instances where either a company outsider like myself, or an HR person with counseling skills, was asked to third-party-broker a disagreement, or to instruct someone in need of additional interpersonal and/or managerial skills. Many companies call this "coaching" and engage in such activities on a wide-scale basis. It's a practice about which I have reservations—not about its usefulness to the individual but its usefulness to the system. I find it valuable when coaching includes a means for upper-level managers to learn what's systemically off that, this time, caused the difficulties necessitating coaching for an individual. In other words, I think every intervention should be scanned for institutional DNA and brought to the attention of company leaders to insure the system benefits from what individuals realize.

Conclusion

I find a preponderance of company leaders falsely impressed, content with company results mainly because they measure up to expectations. I see too many leaders uninterested in what their companies might additionally accomplish from underutilized or mismanaged human capacities. Most leaders conceive their mission as growing their company profitability. They see themselves as strategists, opportunity seekers, problem-solvers, and obstacle-avoiders. They look for facsimiles of themselves in the top-tier managers they employ and don't realize that the biggest internal limitations come from the self-directed ways they and other managers think and behave. Leaders need to accept that it's their job to get this noticed and changed, and I see everyone having a role in helping them figure this out.

No grand solution forthcoming, I've offered a strategy for getting partial solutions and progressing forward from those. I see problems caused by what needs to be addressed but can't be, at least not without wider-ranging awareness. To that end, I've shared my view of the force field in which managers find themselves, and the ensuing dynamics that bog companies down. I hope doing so will make it easier for everyone to more effectively pursue personal and entity goals. I want readers to realize how much rests on a leader's active involvement in getting managers to assume a company-appropriate management mentality. I see everyone's well-being connected to that.

I believe people being forced to pursue their self-interests clandestinely is wrong. I find it an oxymoron when people who have to pretend their interests aren't involved are expected to express themselves authentically. Put self-interests on the table. Make it easier for others to discern whether the enterprise is getting all that it needs. Create the means for people to negotiate their differences. That's what people need to make the most of their companies.

Make it possible for people to be above-board in seeking out win-win-win solutions, where the third win—enterprise accomplishments—is the one that's least compromised. Give people positive reasons to need one another's support. I've seldom heard someone working in a highly successful organization talk about a lack of teamwork, or complain about competition in the ranks. Show me a failing company and I'll bet it's a lack of teamwork that insiders fault most. Get the pretense of objectivity out of daily discussions and all parties will benefit.

Starting out writing this book, my primary goal was to enhance reader awareness. I didn't intend to give nearly as much advice as I eventually did. Going along, I began thinking that readers wanting to involve themselves in a fix could use more guidance. With so much change needed, it'll take every able-minded person to get it done. I see every employee a stakeholder, and every stakeholder interest served by good people realizing more of their good intentions.

When managers evolve their thinking and interact with one another accordingly, work relationships will reconfigure. Interactions with greater authenticity, openness to engaging other people and their different mind-sets, open-minded learning from one's experience, and empathy extended to others—all impractical activities today—should produce additional insights leading to further shifts in mentalities. Then, perhaps a new paradigm for team-play and people being their best will emerge.

Notes

1. G. Vickers, *Freedom in a Rocking Boat* (New York: Basic Books, 1972).
2. Both approaches follow tenets outlined by Paulo Freire in *The Pedagogy of the Oppressed* (New York: Seabury, 1970) and elaborated in a book I authored, *The Organization Trap* (New York: Basic Books, 1974).
3. Also outlined in my book, *Beyond Bullsh*t* (Palo Alto, CA: Stanford University Press, 2008).
4. Termed the "Zeigarnik Effect" after the Russian researcher Bluma Zeigarnik, who performed the initial experiments, and defined in the *Merriam-Webster Medical Dictionary* as "the psychological tendency to remember an uncompleted task rather than a completed one." http://www.merriam-webster.com/medical/Zeigarnik%20effect
5. Martin Winterkorn, who resigned September 24, 2015.
6. Butler, et al. v. Home Depot Inc. No. C-94-4335-SI, 1996, U.S. Dist. LEXIS 3370 (March 25, 1996).

ACKNOWLEDGMENTS

Here's my dilemma: if I were to accurately describe what I went through writing this book, the amount of help I needed and received (I'm not going to), and how many people pitched in over a prolonged period of time, you wouldn't think I deserved much of the credit for writing it. And, given what it took, I don't want people thinking that.

Mark Shahriary is my closest friend, mentor, and therapist. He's also the most intelligent, humane, and thoughtful manager on Planet Earth. I know; I observed him running four companies over a span of twenty years. We meet every Sunday morning at Izzy's Delicatessen for "psyche" sessions tracking the course of one another's lives. That's where, for the last several years, Mark has served as the alter-ego writer of this book. He was there every step of the way—reading drafts, helping me interpret, asking questions, and telling me what I missed. No one could ask for more.

Although we've not met face to face (and that's a story), I count Larry Rout a close and precious friend. We met by happenstance on a writing project, bonded instantly, wrote a book together, and I've been the beneficiary and victim of his genius writing talent ever since. Beneficiary? Because Larry's a generous man and I draw confidence knowing he'll always be there for me. And he has been, time and time again. Victim? Because knowing Larry can always say it better, and in half the number of words, pushes me to be a better writer than I have the stuff to be.

Warren Bennis was my close friend for almost fifty years. We always looked out for one another. He wrote prologues, dust jacket copy, and acted as literary agent for several of my previous books. And he was there at the inception of this book, which for three years prior to his leaving, was an unfolding plot; neither of us had any idea of where it was taking me. I believe Warren would have totally appreciated where I landed—although it's not a place he liked to venture. He was that type of a guy. Warren saw the wonderfulness of leaders and had a keen eye for spotting leadership virtues. My conclusion is the opposite. I see leaders needing to step up and take charge of the tough people stuff, and I see most too self-enamored to do so.

Walter Nord is another dear friend. He's also the most well-read and well-versed scholar I know. I've been surfing the waves of his friendship and insight since we met. I'd tell you the exact number of years but I think Walter plans to work forever and it's probably best that I don't divulge his age. His ideas have impacted my worldview and have greatly emboldened me to write this plain-talking, theory-pushing book. Walter has always had my back. He has my gratitude and love in return.

You can say what you want about your relatives, and I have—some in this book. Among the ones I treasure most is my nephew Paul Koplin. Paul has read, discussed, and reacted to several manuscripts of mine, this one included. I always gain from our conversations and so appreciate his forthrightness and support. This time he gave even more. I faced many personal challenges over the course of writing this book and Paul was always accessible. His father was a wise man. Paul is too.

Henry Dubroff—now there's a natural man. So accomplished, so bright, without pretense and so very humanly accessible. What a favor he did me writing a soulful foreword.

I believe he gave readers the momentum needed to immerse themselves in this book. *O, Henry*, how well you captured what you wrote.

Many people read drafts of this manuscript and were kind enough to share their honest reactions with me. Early drafts were extremely terse and rough, but in most instances not as rough-edged as the grilling I gave my readers. Certainly I value them as glitch-finders and for their supportive praise (I think some people believe I get off on adulation). But I also use manuscript readers as focus-group informants. I sweet-talk them up front and then, increasingly, I begin digging into their experiences and challenging some of what they tell me. If this book had a Hall of Heroes, each of these names would be inscribed on the walls: Reza Kaviani, Scott Schroeder, Ramsey Hanna, Yin Hua, Beverly Kaye, Cliff Burrows, Rossann Williams, Leonard Isenberg, Tom Altura, Jeremy Amen, Joseph Kim, Ilene Kahn Power, Elise Anderson, Matt Inouye, and Ron Pilenzo—and I'm leaving out many whose help I'll never forget but whose names I'm having trouble remembering.

Another person who's very present in this manuscript is Claudia Gilmore Gutierrez. She was my editor at inception and gave momentum to my start. Then she decided to get on with her life—you know, like marriage, and USAID employment in Egypt. Steve Bernhut also helped for a time. I appreciated his goodwill and his diligence in contributing.

The people at Oxford have been fabulous. But it would be a wasted effort mentioning their names. Dedicated professionals, they would say they're merely doing their jobs and edit out any mention of their names. But I think they'll leave in the name of senior editor Abby Gross, who immediately spotted the importance of my message and tastefully contributed to my getting it out. I so appreciate her collaborative spirit and, very important, her willingness to laugh at my jokes—well, most of them.

There are many people I can't acknowledge either for fear of giving away their anonymity or tainting them with discredit for sharing their heretic views. If this is You, thank you very much! The people I can acknowledge are my students, some current and more past, who keep in touch, tell me about their lives at work, and challenge me with the dilemmas they face coping with situations not of their making.

There were four lovely people supporting me with almost-anytime help. They provided the support and interlude conversation that allowed me to focus on my writing. Thank you Silveria Lopez, Joseph Boroumand, Kevin Kurata, and Oscar Garcia.

I saved "my best" for last. Almost from the first day I met her, my wife Rosella has been the best part of my life. I would embarrass you, and her, if I told you the daily sacrifices she made so I could write. Let me leave it at this: there would be no book or Sam Culbert without her. That's as honestly as I can state any fact. She's my life, and I dedicate this book to her with boundless love.

INDEX